Table of contents

The American Girls Guide to Spotting Scumbags, Misfits and Rejects

By

Patrick La Neal

Patrick La Neal

ISBN-13: 978-0692335970 (Custom Universal)
ISBN-10: 0692335978

This book is Dedicated to my loving wife of 25 years who provided me with the wisdom knowledge and understanding needed. I also want to think all my Physicians who kept me alive Dr K Shetye and Dr Maria Gutierrez, My how time has flown. At least long enough to realize this book anyway. Along with the greatest Social Worker in the world at the greatest Dialysis Clinic in the world Davita North Palm Beach. Keep hope alive guy's and Suzanne your the greatest. To my loving sisters who support all my crazy endeavors.

Acknowledgements

All events portrayed inside this book are actual events witnessed. It is important to keep in mind that we have to change the names out for respect to all victims involved in these crimes. Many victim wish to share there stories in this book in hope's that it might save other women from the same fate with the wrong men in the future.

It's a Eye Opening Experience

Listen carefully to what your about to hear

The world of dating is and ever changing world between a man and a woman, or sometimes man and man. Because human beings are such social creatures we crave physical and emotional contact, but some times when we crave these things are we being safe about it. With so many mentally ill and emotionally damaged people out there in the dating world it's become really hard for a woman to established whether or not she's getting some one stable or a psychological wreck. I would honestly like to believe that everyone on-line has good intentions in the dating world, but that's a fantasy and this is the real world. This book is about mistakes, mistake made by people like you and me, some of which who actually lost there lives and others who just barely survived. Its important to never forget how close some of us actually come to certain death and others just creep by. This book is about the dangers of dating and the consequences of falling in love with the wrong person. The truth is as much as I try, I will never be able to tell you ladies everything to look out for. But I will do my best to let you in on the latest scams and cons that are running ah muck these days. When reading this book try to keep and open mind, remember this is not about vampires that blood suckers. It's about that perfect date that just stole your wallet and your identity. It's about that date that went horrible wrong and now he's following you around all over town. It's about the guy that wouldn't take no for and answer, and just slashed your tires last night. It's about the prince charming you took to your parents house who went back a week later and stole you mothers jewelry. This book is not about the good but the bad, its about all the nightmares and the what if's none of you ladies ever think about. But most of all its about safety, and how keene eye's and common sense can make great bed fellows in a crazy world like this. When I set out to write this book I was over whelmed by my life experiences in both corrections and Bail Bonding. The fact is few writers have ever attempted a book like this on such a graphic scale so there's bound to be mistakes. A book that would explain everything from the nature of sexual deviants to human trafficking. From counterfeiting to identity theft, from the latest con and scams to how to move stolen financial data. When I started writing I stopped several times because I realized that in order to keep you ladies up to date on the latest scumbags, I would in fact have to reveal the actual scam itself and in doing so I would risk alerting more scumbags and rejects to a land slide of financial opportunities. The fact is you can't explain the good without the bad so I was forced to put things back into the book and re-write this version, because I had originally edited out and removed many parts from the original version. I put the parts back in to the book about sex trafficking and counterfeiting because it was requested. And a few extra goodie's in hopes that you all would trying to avoid those people. I also put the part in about on-line dating scams because I received a lot of e-mails about that part, especially how to make money as a full time on-line dater. As well, the criminal elements that troll the on-line websites looking for the perfect victim and how they hide themselves within the electronic dating world. When I set out to write this book I convinced myself to write something that would not only alert women to the huge assortment of scumbags, but keep them safe at the same time, which sent me a lot of emailed questions from people like you. Many of you curious and slightly paranoid after the first version. There are many questions I'm often asked in regards to crime and criminals. What makes criminal behavior, How do you spot a criminal behavior, what does a sexual deviant look like and what's the difference between a deviant and a perv. Some have asked me what's the difference between a child molester and a Pedophile and how could you tell whether a man or a woman might be prone to violence or fits of rage. But what maybe my all time favorite what do I do if my spouse starts abusing me physically. These are all great questions and they truly deserve an honest and straight forward answer, and here it is. First let me start by saying, if your looking for someone with a crystal ball that can answer all your questions, and look into the soul of a man or woman stop reading this book. Go and catch the next flight to Thailand, join the nearest monastery and prey for enlightenment. Chances are you'll get all the answers you need before anyone else here does. Truth is their's no crystal ball that can tell us why people do the things they do. I once had a young woman in my custody in the Department place her 6 week old infant in the microwave because of a domestic dispute with her boyfriend. Surely we could all think of a better way to deal with a relationship problem than that, something let's say...more forgiving for the child. But for some strange reason, I have no idea why she commit such a desperate criminal act. For many of us it seems to bend the pole of reason that a person would think that way or even go that far. For that reason, and that reason alone I wrote this book. It's not about emotional malfunctions nor why bad things happen to good people or better yet not even what makes these things happen. I'm not a Ph D, Doctor, Psychologist, neurologist or any kind of medical professional, I'm none of those things. What I am is a person who's spent most of his life dealing with some of the worse criminal type's that society had to offer. And instead of walking away from these rejects or being disgusted by the scumbags I decided to pay attention and listen. To opened one's eye's and mind and pay attention to these people not only to be truly educate, but to be truly enlighten too. I've watched closely over the years, staying close to the pedophile's and scammers, the con artist and the sexual deviants. Many who spend there day's bragging and dreaming about the one's that got away and how many rape's and murder's they got away with, but how they did it and why they did it. You'd be surprised how many serial killers love an audience. I would often ask the tough questions like, Why some pedophiles who see certain types of children get dry mouth or break out in sweats and why others begin to sway back and forth. Some of these are nervous gestures like tapping your feet or to simply sit there and gaze. It took me many years to realize that when these people went on the hunt there juvenile victims didn't see children, they see opportunity. Why do rapist enjoy humiliating and torturing there victims more than having sex with them, why do men who are prone to Domestic Violence take great joy in beating women for total control over them. I mean what exactly are they afraid of? What makes them so tough around women and so cowardly around other men. We spend most of our lives trying to understand what makes these people tick, hoping for signs of some type of chemical in-balance when honestly there is none. What I've discovered in my years is that a young man who starts out as a prick, simply becomes and older prick. These are known as traits or what may many of us regular joe's on the street call tells. Since were not being scientific here, we'll keep it laymen. Now, you'll learn the difference between a sign and a trigger and inside this book we'll go over the difference's in detail. You will learn the difference's between a child molesters and a Pedophile {I.e. The perception of love and hate} but with more detail, something you can understanding and comprehend. We will also discuss simple tactic's they use to lure children, pickup lines, baits and lures and even the kid's they use to recruit your children. Many Sexual Deviants will pay cash to other children to lure your children into the traps they set. You'll learn the best ways to try to prevent this from happening not only by educating your child, but mostly by educating yourself. We'll go into domestic violence and the myth's and stereotype's involved with it, and most importantly why a women may choose to stay with an abusive man even though she has the option to leave. We'll discuss the characteristic's of Domestic Abusers and how to prepare yourself for the bedroom as well as the courtroom. What may ignite certain types of men into becoming physical and if the behavior begins to escalate what are your options. Most importantly why some Police Officers seem not to take domestic violence more seriously and what you can do to convince them otherwise. Truth is the workings of this book is not academics or science but criminal nature in origin. This book is not about Criminal Psychology but the inner workings of a system that's been purposely designed to fail the American people. Domestic violence is tricky and most men who say "I'm sorry I'll will never do it again" are complete liars, and about half of them will actually try to kill you the first opportunity given.

And that's nothing, any women in a Domestic Abuse situation should give serious thought before attempting to leave. Many of these rejects are control freaks and had violent natures from the beginning, many have hired private investigators, lawyers and even cops to track down there missing women. Of course we'll discuss the meaning of off the grid, and how many of you may have no choice but to live off grid in order to survive. So, we'll have to discuss your options and why it maybe harder than you think without the proper training. I'll teach you about *Sex Trolling* (the pickup art's of sex) and the various names associated with the perpetrators within the criminal trade world. There are many known pickup art's in America,many used by various criminal types. Pickups for identity theft, drug trafficking, Cons and *Grifters* (The Art's of Cons) as well as sex. You'll learn the difference between a *John* (A person looking for sex) and a *Chicken Hawk* someone looking for a young boy or teenager to have sex with. And, how thousands of the men busted yearly in these police stings turn out to be married men with families, as well as well respected members of the community. We'll get into sex trafficking of teenagers and why 60,000 runaways a year may not actually be runaways, but kidnappings. We'll discuss how girls and boys who are drugged and kidnapped in one location and quickly moved from city to city sometimes within a matter of hours to work the streets. We'll also discuss how a child missing for more than 24 hours could be two states over in a matter of days, or God forbid inside a crack house turning tricks for some pimp. Many young girls and boys are now working for pimp's who bought them for as little as $300. But have faith, there are times where after you call the cops first   your next call should be to a skip tracer. Police will often have to wait a certain amount of time before they can start looking for missing teenagers they're also bound by laws but skips aren't. Skip tracers specialize in tracking people down who don't want to be found, any and everything you do leaves a trail you just have to find it. But remember every minute you don't call or cooperate with the cops brings you closer to the suspect pool. For many cops it's not about finding the truth, but what they can get a jury to believe. So be careful when speaking to police with regards to information about your family's history, and control yourself you never want to come across as violent natured are angry in a police interview. Remember, in the final equation the truth has nothing to do with it, it's not what you can prove, but what you can convince a jury to believe. This book was designed to be a wake up call for many Parents especially single or divorced women, because the world isn't what it use to be. Many of you are in a constant battle between pier pressure and common sense and common sense is losing. I once had a client who asked me to Bail her boyfriend out of jail after he was arrested for molesting her daughter. The story was the daughter went to school one day complaining of vaginal pain she was only 13 yrs old. Of course this set off a laundry list of flags at the local middle school who called the girl's parent to who was a single mother who basically called her own daughter a liar. Seeing no options, the school had no choice but to call the police. Immediately upon arrival, the police transported the young girl to the hospital for a complete medical exam and rape kit and surprise surprise you guessed it.....yeah!! violated. Needless to say when the police picked our suspect up for interrogation he not only denied the assault but decided to go with the ole "That little bitch seduced me" defense. According to him while he was drunk and passed out, she climb on top and had sex with him. Really... I've been a man all my life... I've been drunk a few times too, but yet to sleep through sex with anybody bouncing on top of me, but let's be honest anything's possible. Later on the investigation would reveal that mom met this Psych job scumbag as a prison pen pal, and started a log term relationship with this jail bird shortly after her husband left her. Needless to say the convict claimed that he was falsely convicted of his previous crime, stating on the night in question he was in church all that night. Funny thing was he had no witnesses. He then claimed his lawyer stuck him and sold him out. Well, not completely uncommon if you dealt with lawyers before, and in the great State of Alabama when your broke, you got a problem. But the fact remains according to the mother, he was a kind hearted gentleman, god fearing, Christian loving man in search of a loving soul. Seems like mom was pretty down on her luck apparently, she had gotten pretty sick after an operation and her husband left her for a younger woman. Sadly she took it hard and begin her own love affair with a bottle of Vicodin. Of course on thing lead to another and a skittles bag assortment of pills. But before you start blaming mom, dad was no masterpiece himself. Not only was he never in the picture for his daughter, but when he was informed as to the sexual assault on his 13 year old little girl he could care less. The investigation would later conclude with the knowledge that the first day the boyfriend was released from prison, he would attempted to have sexually assault the 13 year old child. Yes people as Judge Millian say on the

Peoples Court "You can't make this stuff up". It would also reveal that he had sex with the child several times and in doing so even threatening to kill her mother if the child told anyone about the sexual acts he committed on the girl. Needless to say the pain became to much for her to bare, and the little girl had to tell someone so she told her best friend. And after being confronted about the assault by Police along with several other things, mommy dearest went into a pain pill frenzy and tried to kill herself, clearly the 13 yr old never had a chance. For some reason during the last fifty years we as Americans have under gone some drastic social changes in our lives, mostly in the morality department. The simple fact is that caring about your fellow man is now considered a sign of weakness in our present social and political environment. Seems that most of us have given into pier pressure and have gone in one direction or the other, that is to care or not to care. Some of us set paths that desperately seeking personal financial gain while others seek social exceptance. The question remains, have we just completely stop caring about each other? Most of us are hoping and praying that our train comes in one day, and why not. We all need something to believe in, and shouldn't we all get to live the lifestyle we deserve. Seem's some of us have gone from hard work to scheming to against one another daily all for the sake of collecting a few meager bread crumbs just to keep up with the Jones's. I mean after all is said and done how in the world did trickle down economic's help anyone but the top 3%. And will our kids have the same financial opportunities tomorrow as they do today. Politics has become the number one alienating device of the 21 century bar none. With everyday celebrity voice's flooding the airwaves of our media super highways un-solicited opinions, what will be the next nut bag claim represents the ideal American way of life. Conservative, liberal, independent, progressive, regardless of what you are it's all taken it's toll on our society, our social patience and our personal beliefs, never forget politic's dictate's our punishment. Our perceptions of each other has hit rock bottom, so much in fact, that most of our country's budget thanks to our politicians has started going to other people in other countries. Sadly at the fore front all of this… greed. Our politicians are so busy yelling insults and derogatory remarks at each other that many of us are questioning what actually happen to true democracy. The truth is we've given these clowns way to much power, so much in fact that they no longer bother listening to the people who actually elect them and put them in office. Instead, they give there full attention to any person who writes them the largest check. My father us to say "No one cares when their spending other peoples money" and the truth is he couldn't have been more correct. Every year bad decisions by our elected officials are having a far more of a devastating effect on our society and economy. With global warming if it even exist, at the fore front of many major arguments, and our constitution being shredded before our very eye's what's next.

To Know a Con
Is To See a Con

Let me woo woo woo……cause you should
be mine…..all mine.

Women are often influenced by a handsome man. as well, men are often deeply influenced by a beautiful woman. About 6 years ago I had an client of mine in custody who's specialty was hustling women. He mainly hustled tourist on vacation in the South Florida area and when I say hustle I mean stole everything they had. As he would later go on to explain, he was part of fairly large underground network of well endowed good looking men, who specialized in robbing vacationing women who stayed in 4 or 5 star hotels. For those of you who never heard of this intro.. Jeffery Osborne, Let me woo woo woo you. Yep! many of these women who lay in the sun bathing on our lovely South Florida beaches not only got woo'd…they got robbed too! My job in this book was simple, to tell you not only how it happen but why it happen and what to look out for so it won't happen to you. So, the phrase for today is *Casanova Cretans on the loose.* It starts with a handsome Latino male, deep voice, nice accent walking up to you on the beach. Tall, with his well sculpted bronze body shinning in the south florida sun. As he approach's he say's hello, and you respond back like wise. Then with a nice pleasant voice he say's "Allow me to introduce myself my name Fabio and I'm from Brazil". Now this might be his real name, if your lucky but more that likely it's not. And let's be honest, if you're lucky enough to be on vacation and get introduced to man that looked like that.. who cares. Anyway, you have a few drinks and later he takes you out for a night of dancing under the romantic moonlight. You walk the beach listening to the sounds of the waves crashing along the shore and at the end of the night, a nice romantic kiss. You think to yourself this is going to be an awesome vacation, you run down to the drug store franticly and buy a box of condoms. But what should you get, regular are magnum for the real man. Hey, a girl could dream right? And that's exactly what you doing, DREAMING! This ain't no romance novel this book is about Scumbag, Misfits and Rejects and girl this is a robbery in progress. If your date starts like this you should start looking for the door. So you ask let's go to your place, and he say's "I would but the exterminator just sprayed my apartment for Rats" or better yet the classic "My maid has the weekend off". Now let's be honest, If you ask a man to go to his place and he gives you a bunch of excuses, you obviously have one of two things going on here. 1) He see's you as a total one night stand with no future potential or 2) He doesn't want you to know where he lives because he has bad intentions from to beginning. And as a woman why would you ever go home with a man who had no home to go to. Look when your on vacation, don't bring strangers to your hotel room, the only men that have no home to go to are dead beats and low life loser's. Even serial killers have a place to take women for there entertainment! Look, nobody fly's 2000 miles to shack up with a dead beat on vacation ladies and after you finish reading the rest of this chapter you'll know why. So back to the story. Since your new found Casanova has no apartment and no hotel money you decide to put your romance on hold for tonight. You decide to make plans to spend tomorrow together because he graciously volunteered to show you the town. Luckily for you, he's a perfect gentleman and he volunteers to walk you back to your hotel room, and you gladly except. Two mistakes you made here ladies. First, never take a perfect stranger to your hotel room the first time you meet them. Always say good bye in the lobby, *always,* and never give them your complete name only the first, why? Because very few hotels will allow walk-ins to name phish for for guest (Phish-as in meaning to inquire about or to seek information). Secondly, he now knows your room number, if your next encounter becomes awkward you might have to switch hotels to get away from this creep if he decides to stalk you. This is where it may start to get awkwardly interesting because when you meet your new friend the next morning he walks right up to your room and knocks on your door. Now theres nothing wrong with this but work with me girls, were talking safety here. Anyway, you let him in and right away as he enters he looks your room over, it's like he's never seen a hotel room before. He politely say's nice room and you politely say "Thank you". Of course like the typical woman you're not ready, so you excuse yourself and go to the bathroom for some final touch up's, Bad move again. Never leave a stranger alone with your valuables in your room, there are many women all over the world right now doing 12 year prison sentences for leaving there luggage alone with strangers in Airports. Can you say Drug Mule! So like I said, your date enters your hotel room. Surprisingly to you Fabio seems to knows his luggage, why? because luggage is one way to evaluating the wealth a possible mark for a robbery. High end luggage signals good taste, and good taste is alway a good sign in the robbery business. Afterwards, both of you walk down stairs and head to the beach. When you arrive to the perfect spot on the sand Fabio say's " Why don't you give me your hotel key for safe keeping, you really wouldn't want it to get lost in the sand would you." Not exactly a bad idea but, your momma did give you two of the best purses money can buy. In case you weren't aware of it or by chance forgot they're sitting right on the top of your chest, But reluctantly you agree. About 15 mins later a vendor comes buy selling ice cold drinks and refreshments and quite naturally Fabio offers to buy the refreshments. You ask for something diet of course and Fabio hands that poor broken down vendor a $10 tip. What a generous guy right? Slow down sister cause here's where it gets a little shifty, when Fabio handed that refreshment guy the $10 bill he also handed him your hotel room key. And this is the beginning of what we call <u>The Scoop and Dupe</u>. The dupe and scoop is basically a pickup con that's played by con men and Grifters. This is kid of like the money con, you put a $20 bill on the counter when you pay for your drink, but when the Bartender turns there head you remove it and leave a $10 dollar bill instead, the bartender give's you change for what he thought was a twenty dollar bill and now your ahead of the game. Anyway, turns out Fabio works for a network of Identity thieves who specialize in stealing credit card and passport information and you are about to be there latest victim. There's a stupid belief floating around out there that people who steal your identity will always need the actual credit cards in your wallet. Oh..so untrue my friend, the fact is most of the time they only need a pictures of it. You see you don't actually have to posses the actual cards to charge items on the internet, just pictures of the front and back will do. So while you're on the beach working on your tan lines with your new friend, Fabio's accomplice is now in your hotel room rifling through your personal property inch by inch. Now contrary to popular belief that's not stealing, yes we'll get into crime later. But did you know that every 4 and 5 star hotel has a high end security department at there corporate office's that specializes in protecting it's guest from roaming bands of thieves. These security specialist can monitor the camera system right from there desk at corporate just about any where in the world. This means once there alerted to a possible internal theft problem or room break in they'll normally start searching every digital recording they have on file until they find the perpetrators. This is the difference between staying at the Crowne Plaza and the Roadway Inn. Now most high end theft rings are trained to take pictures of a room before the search it. The object of taking pictures is to allow them to return everything to it's original condition, it also allows you to return home before they start using your cards. That way the suspect pool grows dramatically in size it also includes yourself, your family and friends. The truth is 80% of the time the police are never a threat to these types of rings because there so good at what the do. After taking pictures of all your ID's and credit cards all thats left is returning your room key, which is simple enough. How about some flowers? As you stop buy the flower shop the woman Fabio hands a twenty dollar bill to is also, come on you can guess, that's right part of the scheme. Anyway, as she hands him back his change guess what else she gives him? Thats right, your room key. I'm really not sure who should gets the proper credit for this scam, some say the Italians, others claim the Spaniards but either way it works. My personal belief is if the Italians created it and the Spaniards revised it then the Dominicans Perfected it. Because the bulk of these scheme's are created on the fly, the truth is to love them, you have to understand them. So, let's go to school. When dealing with white collar fraud you need 3 basic things:

1) <u>A Mark-Victim</u>, Fool, Idiot a.k.a a
true Sucker Or someone extremely
Gullible.

2) <u>A Plan</u> - What ever works of course.

3) <u>An Inside man or woman</u>-Someone who
Can gain the trust of all the marks and who
will bring legitimacy to the con.

Once they have your Credit Cards, ID's and Passport information they have 3 options. <u>Turn and Burn</u>, <u>Fabricate and Create</u> or <u>Third party Wholesale</u>. So let's Look at turn and burn.

<u>Turn and burn</u> is just what it say's. Let's say someone drops there wallet in front of you and instead of telling them you pick it up and start spending. My friend you just pulled a basic Turn and Burn. You immediately went on a shopping spree burning as much credit and cash as you can. But if you plan on staying out of jail I would suggest you find a drunk or better yet a crack head to do the spending for you. However, this may prove to be difficult when trying to spend money on the internet because it's only a matter of time before the person that dropped the wallet realizes it's gone. Therefore where ever you go has to be anonymous or you need a pigeon. Like I said some homeless person or drug addict to blaze the cards for you.

<u>Fabricate and Create</u>, Capitalism is a bitch and thanks to those corrupt greedy American Corporations that make those Credit Card making machines, duplicate cards are only a mouse click away. If you throw in your Chinese business who will gladly sell you anything you want as long as it's on-line and you got the cash.

Creating fresh credit cards from scratch is as easy as baking a pie. Since the Chinese have started counterfeiting every known type of business machine known to America, not to mention the fact they manufacture most of them all anyway, it's like shopping at Walmart. Honestly there's truly nothing out of reach of the average everyday criminal. I once went to a clients house that I bailed out of jail on a drug charge to collect the balance he owed on his Bond. When I walked in to the house I saw this big computer like machine sitting on the table. I asked "What the hell is that" he smiled proudly and said "That's a drivers license machine, it's used for creating fake Drivers licenses. And just think, if you were one of those people who believed rehabilitation works, sucker! Apparently they'd been saving for month's to go into a brand new business, the counterfeiting business. There main source of income was creating fresh ID's from stolen Identity's they had, and all of which had legitimate starts. Most of these ID's were stolen from dates with unsuspecting women and men without there knowledge. This way when they copy and forge checks there automatically link to legitimate people with legitimate bank accounts. Just the ID's were fake. The problem is Check Cards, with check cards it's became much harder to kit and steal paper checks. But good news, today's criminals have learn to adjusted and have started trading in ID machine's for Credit Card machines.

<u>Wholesale-The</u> last ditch effort of a desperate criminal will always be uploading Credit Card numbers to a universal Mainframe to sale on the net. Anyone with a little cash and access to the Hackers Underground can get access to these numbers. The Nigerians have perfected this uploading thing on to foreign servers because it gives them anonymity. But right now as we speak the Russians have become the number one cybercrime hoods in the world. The truth is that some white collar crimes still require a personal touch, and the Con is one that always will. As a woman you should alway's be Leary of things and people that sound to good to be true, and keep your eye's open always. I'm not saying that you shouldn't have fun, but you shouldn't get swept up in the moment before thinking of what it could cost you. So let's recap on our vacation rules shall we:

1) When ever you plan on leaving important documents behind in hotels such as purses, passports, Credit cards, Jewelry and cash always use the hotel safe. Any protection is better than just leaving

your stuff laying around. You should always remember as Americans that we are often targets in many part's of the world. Not only do you have to look out for the Cons but the Maids too.

2) It's not robbery if you give someone your keys, remember the way conservative's think about fraud, it's always your fault. When it come's to fraud and scams the law is rarely on your side, that's why it's one of the hardest conviction for a prosecutor to win. Don't let a heat of the moment decision strand you in a foreign country you know nothing about.

3) Use the purse your momma gave you when you leave to go out on informal day trips. This makes you less of target with purse snatchers and pick pockets especially in Europe.

4) Make sure you call someone back home at least once a day to tell them where your heading next when traveling, at least it will give someone and idea where to start looking if something go's wrong.

5) Never get into vehicle with strange men you don't know, especially when your out numbered and traveling alone. Always try to hook up with a buddy.

6) Stick with hotels with 4 or 5 star ratings, most criminal elements can't afford to do business out of places like this so your less likely to run into riff raff.

Remember this book is designed around Scumbags, Misfits and Rejects so what ever we discuss in this book is for the purpose of protecting yourself from them... good luck.

The Devils not watching you......he's here!

To Expect the unexpected

For the last twenty years are so the United States has undergone and explosion of foreign invaders, some of which are nothing less than questionable. As a think back about my last twenty years of dealing with Creeps, Cretans, Crazy's and Sociopaths, I am often reminded of just how many of these guys where foreigners. When women choose to fall in love with men from other countries, they sometimes align themselves with some pretty shifty characters. Not that we don't have plenty of losers in America too! But it's pretty easy to find out information on just about any American with a legitimate social security number. But if you do decide to date a foreigner, have you ever stop to asked yourself's how would you find out what kind of person your dating from Ukraine or Dubai or for that matter any other country. The truth is trusting people these day could get you killed. I once had an inmate in my custody who was actually from the Ukraine, good looking guy too. Unfortunately he was doing a 8 years sentence for human trafficking. What caught my attention about him and his case was whenever his American girl friend came to visit him in jail she alway's left frantically crying. Now just so you know most of the time during any visitation process they'll always be a little crying on both sides of the table. That being the inmate's side and the visitors side. But I would later determine that she had a child with this inmate and the inmate was threatening to have his family come kidnapped the child. Seems that if she ever stop sending him money or fail to come visit him he would have his family come and steal the child and take it back to the Ukraine. She would later go on to say that if that happen she would lose all her right's to her child and would more than likely never she her child again. I couldn't help but wonder why someone would take his own child and send it back to some third world war ridden village. However the answer my friend would soon reveal itself, and this one did't shock me. You see our inmate friend was nothing more than a Ukrainian criminal who once his sentence was complete would be deported back to his home land. Which meant he couldn't return to America unless of course he was married to an American citizen. Yeah, love may be bliss all right but blackmail isn't, I truly felt sorry for this woman. Seems behind door one was the loss of your only child and behind door two a life with a foreign scumbag who would never be truly out of you life. To make matters worse there's something that most women rarely think of when dating foreigners, and that's the culture gap. This could not only makes the relationship difficult, but could also make the entire situation down right dangerous because of unknown customs that may be involved. You see, in some cultures through out the world women are considered nothing more than second class citizens with no right's at all. This normally proves very difficult for an American woman and could prove to be a real problem. Especially when an American woman falls in love with someone say from the Muslim region or even worse Western Europe. You see the laws in these countries provide little help for woman more-less Americans in a legal sense, and trying to operate within there court system as an American could be total waste of time. But while you may be dazzled by Romeo's good looks and accent, you may what to remember one thing. If Romeo was and American and committed a crime you would at least have the justice system to fall back on, though as not a perfect system it's still something. But think about this, if your Romeo and you were walking down the street arm in arm and he were to suddenly become angry and let's say stab you, what would you do? I mean right now, this very minute if he decided to violently attack you what would happen to him. You could call the police and press charges, but remember Romeo has one advantage that no American guy has, he could leave the country. Think about it, all he has to do is get to the airport before the police discover who he really is and he's gone. How is it that none of you people ever think about this until something like this happens? Anyone can gain access to the United States as long as you have two thing's. Connections and Money no Passport needed. I know one Mexican guy who was arrested 5 times with five different aliases and because the Feds took so long to find out who he was he alway's made bail. He simply goes back to Mexico pay's a corrupt official for a new identity and a month later he's back. Now all the fake identity's in the world won't change his finger prints, but running finger prints take time. It's especially difficult when they go to a different city every time they cross the border. The fact is foreign men have the means of not only changing there identity's but depending on what part of the world there from, even there origin. Most countries in South America allow people to freely travel from one country to the other. Just because he says he's from Argentina doesn't mean he's actually from Argentina. No differently than him claiming he's from Nashville but actually growing up in Detroit. The major deference were talking about here folks is safety, what do you know about him, and what can you find out about him. If he's American and he's using a fake name or social that's not hard to find. If he's from Romania and he's using a fake name then where the hell do you begin. The first time my wife and I went to New York City and saw Brighton Beach and I asked myself " Where in the world did all these Russian people come from. Considering the fact that Organized crime is at an all time high I can only imagine, but where does that leave us as Americans. Our two party system sucks and seems to be stuck on stupid. One party keeps trying to destroy the Government and the other wants to make it responsible for everything. And as always caught in the middle, the American tax payer. Who for some strange reason is constantly on the losing end of this game. What I'm simply trying to say is you can't depend on anyone to protect you but you, and I'm constantly preaching this to you women. You women have simply become way to trusting period.

Many of you feel that you owe it to yourselves to simply save some guy like a lost or stray puppy, but the truth is for men it's sink or swim. And you know what, that's the way it should be because men are creatures of habit. For most men If you allow them to sleep on your couch, eat your food and then give them the bonus of having sex they'll never leave, they'll never work and they'll never aspire to do anything. Not if he knows your paying the bill for everything. If you throw in the culture clashes of other countries it's a toxic mix that could makes it very difficult to not only understand but, to even except so take your time to get to know someone. Here's some important pointers when attempting to date foreigners:

**When meeting someone from a foreign country take it slow, Most Foreign cultures believe American women are these skimpy dress sluts that put out at the drop of a hat. The words " I love you " are some kind of magic potion to an American women's heart, Hey.. make them work for it!

**Never share your fiancees with foreigners more less any man you just meet, can you say terrorist watch list. Don't deposit any strange checks or open any accounts or even cosign for any credit. Never accept any sudden marriage proposals nothing like finding out the hard way you're wife number 7 and the other 6 will be moving in next week. And just so you know the higher your number on the wife ladder the lower you are on the totem pole.

**Don't agree to let there friends stay in your home or allow them to move-in any relatives, It's best to be on the safe side initially. I once spoke with an immigration officer that told me that some foreign scammers give classes on beating the American system, Welfare food stamps you name it they can more than likely get it. It's to bad as an Americans we can't.

**When having sex always use protection this goes for foreign and domestic men but emphasis on foreign especially African and Third word regions. There are some things that soap won't wash off. If you know what I mean.

Now we get to the hard stuff so here we go. When dealing with cultural diversity certain bad habit's come with certain cultures and violence towards women is one of those cultural things. If your dealing with men from the Middle Eastern regions women are expected to be more servants than wives. The simply phrase "Do as I say an not as I do" carries a totally different meaning in some cultures so be careful. There are thousands of women that are trapped in marriages of servitude where fear is the main motivation. To complicate matters are the children, there's nothing worse than some Foreigner knocking you up and leaving you for months on end, only to return to his home country and leaving you with all the expense. What's even worse, is to finding out he has five more wives in five different country's. Trust me I met a woman that this happen to, she tried to get a divorce from this jerk and the guy sued her. Remember someone traveling on a student visa has restrictions and is a lot different from someone traveling on a Business visa. Keeping this in mind it's a lot easier for the

Business type of scumbag to carry on multiple lives with multiple women in multiple places. Another fact is most women are more prone to accepting Domestic Violence when children are involved, but having it done by foreign nationals does tend to complicate the situation. Like I mention earlier blackmailing for the purpose's of maintaining custody of the children is quite common especially when breaks ups are ugly. You should consider all of this things before bedding down with any man, but pay special attention with foreigners. If you do however have a situation where this could happen, you should weigh on the side of caution. Remember as an American you may not be welcomed with open arms in his home country and the chance's of you being trick or scammed are pretty high. Not knowing the lay of the land can be hard on anyone not to mention throwing in a foreign language. If you haven't noticed a pattern by now it should be obvious, Kids are the ultimate weapon of choice by foreigners. Many foreign men believe American women are spoiled and need to be thought a lesson, or at least the ones I've been around. I know a lot of guy's in South Florida from the Islands who use women for everything there worth. Later they leave many of them in such debt that most can never recover. Remember a man with nothing has nothing to lose, so anything he gets from you puts him that much ahead of the game. Make sure when your dating these guy's to take your heart off your sleeve because if they see it, they'll take it. Your identity is the most important thing you have as an America citizen and before taking someone else's name you should know the baggage that's accompanying it. Finally, research the culture of the individual your dating, make sure to the best of your ability that he is who he say's he is. Don't let any man persuade you to do something stupid, so we'll go over the most common criminal acts:

** Look, I have and extra bag and there's a limit at the airport could you check this in for me under your name. Hell No! I don't care how good the sex was. Instead of thinking sex think time, 10-20 years in prison, better safe than sorry.

** Things are so much better in my country, you'll love it there. You can sell everything you own here and come to live with me in my country. People, You have know idea how many women will pack there bags and fly off to some mosquito ridden jungle just because some guy told them so. The real question is if thing's are so good where he came from, why is he here? What's worse most women are so embarrassed when they find out they've been hoodwinked that there reluctant to return home. Don't be a fool everyone makes mistakes just make sure you learn from it. They call them whirl wind romances for a reason ladies, try using a little more common sense.

** Never give up your American citizenship
for anybody.

** When in a foreign country, beware of the flashy men types, you know the " I know a place, trust me" type of guys. I've traveled all over and let's be honest people the "I know a place" guys have always been nothing but trouble. Any man you just met that say's "trust me" is like the guy that use's god and money in the same sentence. And everybody who reads the bible know's you don't ask god for money you ask for blessings.

Gee….I didn't see That coming

The story of the obsessive compulsive Man

One of my favorite comedians is a guy by the name of Jeff fox worthy who has a routine many of us have come to love. The infamous "You might be a redneck if " is one of the most popular routines ever. Now it may shock many of you out there just how few women actually know what an obsessive man is. So here and now I will begin to layout the most familiar traits of an obsessive man and what you can look forward to for your entire marriage.

You might have an obsessive compulsive
Man A.K.A a selfish Piece of crap if?

1) Everything within your world has to go
His Way.

2) His opinion is the only opinion that
Matters.

3) When his woman has a bright idea, she
Naturally stole from him.

4) Every other word is "I told you so".

5) When his wife is a total idiot for not
asking for permission first for anything.

6) When sex last less than a minute and
when He's finished he rolls over and goes
to sleep as though nothing ever happen.

7) When you say "We need to talk" he
Immediately changes the subject.

8) When everything you want to buy is a
Waste of money and everything he wants
to buys is a necessity.

If you experiencing any of these while dating a man let's be frank when I say "Girl run… you ain't gone yet". Women often set themselves up for failure by ignoring the warning signs, I mean if your under the expression that you can change a man your a fool. Your job as a woman is not to re-raise a man that's already been raised by his momma. There nothing worst for a woman than to have to raise a man and his children at the same time, really… it's just to much. Learning the warning signs well before you fall in love with this jerk could be a life saver for any woman but first recognize the signs. I once knew a guy so possessive that he picked the brand of feminine pads his wife wore. The same guy would on occasion come home throw a tantrum expressing how stupid his wife was and how much of a mistake he made by marrying her. Many people would say that it was just his way of showing love, but really he was a 2 timing piece of crap who wanted to know where his wife was always. On the street pimps call this flipping a bitch.

The purpose of flipping a bitch is to crush a woman's spirits, you want her to learn that the only opinion in the world that matters is yours, the only world that exist is yours and the only words she should ever hear are yours. By reprogramming a woman psyche the man basic controls how a woman process information, not from him of course, but from others. The breaking down of a woman's soul and spirit is important for domestic abusers because most of them are majorly insecure. Any woman that's prone to challenging his authority must be dealt with quickly and harshly, due simply because she his wife, may actually start making her own decisions. And this my friend is what we call free will. There are basically three popular ways of handcuffing a woman a.k.a keeping your woman in check when it comes to these types of guy's:

1) <u>Religion and the Bible-A</u> woman should
obey the words of a man no matter what?
The Bible has always been a true weapon of
right wing domestic abusers because
conservative family's often Raise there
daughter's to follow the Teachings of God.
Un-fortunately with the wrong guy these
can sometimes get you killed.

2) <u>Isolation No contact-No</u> friends, No family, No phone calls and No money means No competition. When you strip a woman of means you basically make her totally dependent on her man and this is what they want. Think of it this way, if your responsible for feeding your children and you suddenly stop what happens…. They starve. You get the picture.

3) <u>Physical contact and Mental abuse-unfortunately</u> our laws were created by corrupt men and women. The simple fact is our laws have not grown up with the times and there are many who

feel that verbal abuse is not actually abuse but free speech. As the F.C.C puts it "You can be offensive but not obscene". And whats the old saying "sticks and stones may break my bones but names will never hurt me". Thats the biggest crock of crap I've ever heard, not only could it hurt you, it can kill you. I'm sure there's a couple of kids at a certain high school in Columbine, CO, that would totally disagree with you. I'm pretty sure when they woke up that morning for school, many of them never thought they'd be dodging bullets. Just because someone doesn't touch you doesn't mean there's not abuse, again this has nothing to do with common sense but totally and completely with politics. Many years ago I volunteered to attend a woman's abuse clinic by a dear friend of mine.

I was very reluctant because I felt I had nothing to offer, boy was I wrong. As some of the stories of torture emerged I was shock. Not at what they experienced, but just how creative some of the methods of torture were. I mean there are really some sadistic men out there who really get off on torturing their women daily. But one thing came up most often as I attended these meetings and that was of course gay men in the closet. How can you tell if you married a man that's hiding his sexuality in the closet, there are many women who believe that a gay man could never have sex with women. Bullcrap! I've seen guys in work release go on furloughs with there wives for 8 hours and comeback to the center and have oral sex with a man in the same day. How? Who knows but they just can. So much so that many after release continue there affairs on the side without there wives having any idea there meeting another man. And believe me when wives first discover this most of them lose it, some will go as far as retaliation, but I'm here to tell you your just making a mistake. These men all have one thing in common, there all living their lives as complete and utter liars. Think about it, how hard is it to have sex with a women telling her you lover her and the whole time being in love with another man. Wow! talk about fraud..please it's the ultimate betrayal.

And yes while your reading this book a lot of you are wondering, and many of you have no idea that about 16% of you are married to closet Homosexuals. Yeah just that many! You see, when men go to prison not every man is raped, many actually volunteer themselves to make there lives easier. And for many years I've often wondered, why? Prostitute's rarely volunteer to go to a street corner to turn tricks, They go because they have to or there addicts and it's mainly done out of desperation. But when a man come's to prison and finds himself relieved to be their and right at home, well thats a totally different story. Most homosexuals in prison are treated like royalty, especially when they establish there sexual orientation up front. The truth is in prison there known as <u>Master-cards</u>. Please don't let me have to go into the gory details I'm sure you know what I mean. The flip side is if they try to hide it well however, many do find out the hard way. Most of these people will do anything to keep there secret a secret so be careful and tread lightly and don't threaten. Try not to over react and cause a scene, I want to see all of you live just a little bit longer if you know what I mean. And if this does happen to you try to divorce with dignity, and not being vengeful. This believe it or not goes totally against the healing process. Many women will often take it pretty hard and never trust another man again, but believe me you're not alone with this one and believe it or not you'll live.

The sooner most of these men accept responsibility for there lie's and false deceptions, the better off everyone involved will be. Simply put, you are what you are. Personally, I've always found it to be the hardest on the kids, thats why maintaining a calm demeanor is very important. But back to the subject.... What you didn't see coming. The truth is what you don't see can and will hurt you, just how much no one really knows. I can tell you that you should always make sure what you see is what you get when it comes to a man or woman that's important. But this doesn't mean if he isn't truthful and turns out to be a fraud sexually, he's not capable of some really good things. Men are always in a hurry to do things without thinking it through completely, there's a part in the Bible that basically says "only a woman is capable of unconditional love" but truthfully that doesn't mean she'll give it to you. Men on the other hand will have conditions for everything, anything a man does in this world will have a conditions attached, which explains why men have no problem packing up and walking away at the drop of a dime. Women must first except this condition, but realizing at the same time that not every man has this horrible trait. Anytime a man comes into a relationship and presents a laundry list of conditions for maintaining that relationship will alway's be a bad sign.

The fact that certain request must be fulfill before he'll do anything for you as his woman, is a definite sign that you should seek life else where. Why? Because It's really hard to complain about something in a marriage that was there in the marriage 10 years ago when you first started dating. If you let it go on for 10 years believe me it's your fault don't blame him, you have to take some of the responsibility for your actions as well as his. Men are Apex Predators, they'll always seek the path of least resistance, this means they'll always flock to women that give them what ever they want when they want it. Back in the old days it was common for a man to court a woman for a substantial amount of time before having sex with her. But nowaday's if she doesn't put out by the third date she suddenly a casualty of war. The truth is I have no idea what happen to men, but I agree with a lot of women when the say "It's pretty scary out there".

What's wrong with Women

Maybe it's what your looking for that's the Problem

Most women have there own perception of what the ideal man should be. Some say tall dark and handsome, others say tall with blue eye's, some will tell you a gentle soul with sensitive feelings. Some might go as far as needing a man that they can relate to them on a personal level. Others may just want a man as a solid provider that's low demand and low maintenance. And you know what? I think your all crazy, because honestly none of you really know what you want. Why else would you say "It's a woman's prerogative to change her mind" I mean who say's that. When I was working at the woman's shelter, I would listen to some of the women describe in detail there otter failures in relationships with men.

And every time I heard a women complain about there relationship with a man it would alway's occur to me that women seldom practice what the preach. They all have laundry list of expectations and only then do they settle for the first thing that walks by with a great body and a sparkling smile. The fact is understanding woman is a lot like understanding the rules of culinary school, most importantly "You eat with your eye's first, and if it doesn't look good you'll never get my attention". And at a certain time in a man's life, everyone knows ladies that you ladies love to eat with your eyes. But to understand women is to understand the main question, do women create there own problems, and yes I think it's an honest and legitimate question. Simply put, when it comes to relationships with men, all women will eventually settle for less and my not realize it. But the real question that women often ask about men is, "Are all men genetically prone to being scumbags, Misfits and Rejects?" First, lets look at women. Is it possible that you actually created a Scumbag or Misfit by giving into his demand constantly clearly when you honestly should've held your ground on a matter? Here's a true story. When I was in high school every girl I was interested in was never interested in me. For some reason every babe I had a crush on wanted a guy with a new car, and an American Express card. He had to be as sensitive as Michael Jackson but able to draw first blood like Rambo. It wasn't until I got in may 20's that I realize the truth, that beauty is in the eyes of the beholder. The fact that all the girls I knew in High School wanted someone with a body like chiseled stone and a bank account like Donald Trump was a sign that I should move on to greener pastures. It was there at the top of Mt Totally confused that I realized that I had to be freck'in crazy. I was listening to a bunch of crazy chic's that had no clue what they wanted in a man as well as life. So, instead of trying to be like mike, I would try to be like Chuck. Yeah Chuck! You see, my cousin Chuck wasn't this tall dark and handsome guy, come to think of it he was only 5'6 and in the looks department well, let's just say when god was handing out good looks he was in the bathroom. My cousin had coke bottle glasses that were so thick that I swear to God one day we were outside reading comic books and the sunlight shining through his glasses actually caught the page's on fire. No bullshit! That comic book actually lit up like a barn fire. But wait ladies, here's the thing, what my cousin lacked in the looks department he instantly made up for in Penis Department. You see, my cousin was hung like a rhino in a rain forest, oh yeah girls, he had the goods. Back when we were little his nickname was Mr Magoo, but after high school the women gave him a new name "The Womb Wrecker". Yes, people my cousin was the stud of the neighborhood, and maybe even the decade. And how the hell did that happen? Who knows, better yet who cares, but there was one thing for sure, he was getting more ass than all the benches in the Food Stamp Office. I mean he was the man, which was even more puzzling to me, who would think when you sign up for a dating site how many would ask for length. Anyway, as I would later learn my cousin was a total stud muffin which thought me something important about women and what they were looking for in men. A entirely different list of requirements that they actually keep to themselves. So here's a list of the most <u>confusing</u> classics.

1) Bad boys- You know, that ruff tuff and tumble type, the kind the slaps you around and steals your car.

2) A man that's aggressive-You know the kind, the one's you take home to momma's house and he comes back two days later and robs her house.

3) The type of man that dress good and drives a nice car- Oh god he's so Hot! My My, It must have been a huge shock to discover he lives at home and that's actually his daddy's car.

4) He has to be a real good listener- Who knew he was smoking marijuana and was high the whole time, no wonder he laughed at all your jokes.

Back to the story. Now honestly my cousin only met one of those criteria which was he smoked marijuana daily, and at a certain point in his life he actually stop working because it inter feared with his time to get high. But that never stopped my Kuz, no way he was so hung his ladies gave him and allowance, true story. In fact he stopped having sex with all woman under 40, why, because there was no money in it. His bedroom game was so good that once he threaten to leave one of his high priced honey's. In fact one night she threaten to kill herself by laying in the middle of the road and waiting to be hit by a on coming car. My cousin turned his high priced 1982 BMX bicycle around, rode up to her, looked down and said "Scoot over more to the left, your not quite in the middle of the road yet". After 23 years of living and seeing that, one thing occur to me that instant, I realized that my cousin was a Real Mac Daddy. No love, no guilt, no remorse no nothing. And by the way would you like to know why my cousin was breaking up with this lady? Because he wanted a raise in his allowance and she said no, She actually said she couldn't afford it. She went on to say she had to pay for her daughter's college tuition, my cousin told her "It's me or your daughter" but needless to say 2 weeks later she called my cousin to say she made her daughter get a job. Wow baby! Now that's penis power. I wanted to know what makes a woman give that kind of control to a man, and that kind of control over her life and others in it. The fact does however remain, that one could actually consider this a form of abuse, all though not violent in nature the withholding of affection itself could be considered a form of abusive. When I was 23 I never took the time to ask these questions, If someone withheld affections from you how would you respond? Especially if you loved that person deeply. I was only 23 years old then and quite frankly didn't care. But this is what most of you women can look forward to when dealing with these type's of guy's in the future:

1) <u>Bad boys may make the best lovers</u> so they say which may explain why so many of you woke up with your purses missing the next morning along with your cash and jewelry. Seems every girl I talked to in high school that went for the bad boy ended up broke, abused or Pregnant. Gotta love those bad boy's, but there's some good news for those of you ladies who fell victim to those bad boys… the trend continues.

2) <u>An aggressive man who knows what he wants</u> and goes after it. Unfortunately ladies Bank Robbery doesn't count, neither does kidnapping, burglary or armed robbery just so you know.

3) <u>Dressed good and drove a nice car</u>- One of the biggest crimes against women in 2012 was Identity theft. Seems many of you after having hot passionate sex with these rejects handed over all your

personal information. The rest of you after breaking up with your heavenly hunks of "I wish I'd never met you" forgot to change the passwords on your computers and email accounts. Why in god's name would you ever give any man you barely know your personal information. Honestly?????

Sensitive and good listener- Nothing wrong with that, just remember Ted Bundy was a real sensitive guy too, and he listen to all his women, just before he cut their heads off. You should work harder to make sure he's listening to you, and not listening out for the cops!

This of course brings me to another eye witness account story. Hey Stop it, you bought this book so gonna listen. This story involves one of the patients at one of my former dialysis centers. I'll call her Josie which of course is not her real name, but I do make every effort to protect the victims. When I first saw her with this guy I thought "WoW… What's wrong with this picture" this guy was about 6′2, slim and with a great smile that made Enrique Iglesias look like a crack head. I mean this guy was physically ripped and cut like a kilo of cocaine by a Jewish drug dealer. And, he had the looks to match which of course made him the total package ladies. On the other hand Josie was just an average looking woman who was roughly about 10 years his senior, she was quiet, shy and somewhat reserved not quite the women you'd expect with this guy. For me everything about this guy screamed moocher, but then again who was I to Judge. But one day when she came into the clinic for treatment, she was crying her eyes out like it was the end of the world and her refrigerator was empty. I knew then what ever it was it had to be bad. As she went into telling the story of what happened something started sounding so eerily familiar about this M.O (Method of Operation). Yeah, it's like I've heard this story a hundred times at the woman's shelter. And being in the Bail bond business I've meet a many of men like this, but it's not what he did, but how he did it that was so intriguing to me. Seems her boy friend went into her bank account on her computer before leaving town and did what was known as a Personal Bill Pay Con. So what's is personal bill con you ask? Well I thought you'd never ask. Most banks offer something called Personal bill services to there customers through on-line banking, simple put, they write the checks to you creditors for you. You just setup the name of the creditor and the date you want the bill paid and the amount, and presto the bill gets paid. This allows the customer to send monthly checks to people without ever leaving there home, which is good for Kidney Patients like us because Dialysis often leaves us totally drained and weak. But it's not just the crime but how he did the crime thats actually quite genius. He had the checks mailed to various P.O boxes through out the county under various names all in all about $3500.00. And he not only attacked her checking but her savings as well, along with a few minor shopping spree's with her credit cards a long the way. When he was done with her and her finances he just vanished, Disappeared, no call, no note just upped and gone. She often spoke of this guy like she trusted him with her life saying "If it wasn't for Juan I don't know what I'd do". Well if I could turn back the hands of time is one of my all time favorite song's by Sam Cooke, but honestly I doubt if she'd want to hear it. So without further delay here's the best way for a single woman or married woman out on the town to protect herself.

1) Never give anyone your personal information, this includes pin numbers, social security numbers and family history. Why family history? Because most security questions ask for for some type of family info like mothers maiden name, first dog, first car, high school mascot and e.t.c.

2) Lock your personal computer's and laptop's with passwords, I know it's tempting when someone ask "Can I use your computer

for a second" but the truth is you can always say it's broken or it has a virus and I haven't taken it in for servicing yet. This way if they try to power it up while your not around they'll have a harder time getting pass the initial encryption. And make sure if have company, shut it down completely just before you start entertaining.

3) When going out a night to clubs, theaters or any place of a social gathering, always use the buddy system and never separate from each other. I know this sounds stupid but if there's more than 3 guy's and 2 of you, there far less likely to try something shifty. Another thing is to use your natural purse for you personal items, no.. not your Coach, but the natural purse that your momma gave you, you know those two spotlights on up top your chest your so proud of. There not only good for showing off pasties, but great for concealing things too so use them for stuff like your I.D's and at least one credit card. And always carry cash, at least fifty bucks in case your date dumps you out on the road. Or better yet if you don't agree to put out for him or have sex with his buddies or you just find him plain ole creepy. Sleeping with someone will always be your prerogative, and never forget it! You should never feel as

though you're under pressure, it's not date rape, It's a date and your consent needs to be completely implied.

4) When ever your out with a total stranger's Never..I mean Never.. I mean EVER..walk away from any drink or beverage and return to continue to drinking that same beverage. And let me be frank the same applies to your food too. I've had several inmates in my custody that specialized in spiking and lacing the drinks and food of women so be smart.

5) Never assume because a man is ordering drinks from the bar for you and your girl friend that he's actually paying for them, he may not have a dime to his name so don't get caught with this one. Grifters will often latch on to the popular girls in a Night Club just to juice up there tabs and leave. I've seen many babe's get stuck with somebody else's tab at the end of the night so going dutch sometimes is the best way to go otherwise you might need bail money.

6) Never lend a stranger your cell phone! This has got to be what my father called " The Elephant's ass of stupid" Of course he was from South Carolina where they say things like that. But it's the

security aspect of the situation that worries me. Once a person has access to your phone and number they can install just about any piece of spyware available on the market, even tracking spyware. Hackers are everywhere so please be careful and protect yourself.

7) Never believe once a horrible date is over at the end of the night that your done with that guy. Psycho's have a powerful residue they leave behind, so one thing I will always suggest is after any horrible date take a break for at least 2 weeks? Why? Because if he's a mental case or a nut bag he might actually be following you around town. It's important after these dates to switch up your routine a little. If you walk to work stop at a coffee shop and look for familiar faces. Leave a little early in the morning's just to make sure the losers not tailing you, and if he does make contact afterwards make sure he's not volatile. If he is go to into the nearest place of business and tell them your being followed by some creep. The reasoning behind this is if god forbid something happens to you, hopeful whom ever you pointed this guy out to might be stand up enough to remember. The other reason is it's much easier to catch the creep on the business's security camera's and now the cops know who to look for. But truthfully, only go to a male attendant if there's no female attendant in the store. Some men tend

not want to get involved in awkward situations with other men, and are not receptive if a frantic woman runs in off the streets so stay calm.

8) The mirror in your car is for more than just lipstick. Use it to be more observant when your driving. Most stalkers don't do random, so when your talking about stalkers and kidnapping most of these guy's plan things out in advance.

For the most part dating can be fun but try to make it safe too, remember we live in a world where the men are becoming a little more stranger each day. And honestly these day you need to remain on your toes. Even at a young age boys have no concept of the proper way to woo a girl, here's another example…oh please. A friend of mine in South Florida has a daughter who's 14 years old that was asked out on a date by a 14 year old boy or so he thought. Now my buddy wasn't to keen on the idea of his daughter dating at such a young age but he was over ruled by his wife. Now this created a riff between him and his wife, so the wife decided to use this as leverage against the father towards the daughter. Never the less he finally gave in after the daughter continued to use his wife's words against him. So he agreed, but only if he went along on the date and that he said was non-negotiable. When he arrived with his daughter to the movie theater, the date was already there and waiting. But believe it or not the kid had no money, zip, nada, totally tapped out I mean nothing in his pockets folks. Now according to my buddy, he was so insulted by this that he threaten to take his daughter back home when his daughter blurted out "Dad I have money". What! he said. Quite naturally he then asked the obvious "who asked who out here" and his daughter said "I asked him". Now for me as a father, how would you handle something like that, in fact the kid was so obviously defiant that he just stood there and smiled at my buddy. Truthfully when the date was over, the kid actually paid for nothing the entire night, and my friends daughter paid for everything.

But what really pissed him off was that the entire night all the kid kept doing was looking back at him and laughing, it was completely disrespectful. It's now becoming ever so clear that boy's these day's are being raised with a total lack of respect for women. And the scary part is it's actually women that are pushing the cause for this change. Sorry ladies, I hate to say it but your doing it to yourselves. luckily I had a son, and even though he was an only child I'd hope he'd always show consideration to any woman he felt interested in. After all he knows my motto "Treat others like you want to be treated, unless the treat you like shit then treat them the same as they treat you". I have 2 little nieces whom I love to death and I often wonder what kind of men they'll attract in the future. You know, I've been saving money for by Brother in-laws bail because I know his day's coming soon, I got your back Jimmy. And honestly, are there any young african American males right now being raised properly enough that'll actually be worth a dam for them. And something else, have women in the twenty first century just become so desperate for a man that they no longer have any standards. And if so, will this so call conservative movement handicap most of them to the point where there opinions no longer exists or even matter.

I mean it's becoming quite clear in some aspect's that the barefoot and pregnant wife movement is slowly coming back into play. What's even worst is god forbid if one of them does get assaulted by some sexual deviant will they still have the options that a women needs to have. Don't get me wrong I understand the religious implications but religion like everything else in America should always be a choice. I believe it to be the right of the individual not the government..period.

10 Signs your better off alone

Because you can do bad all by yourself

As I stated earlier I spend some time early in my career speaking to women of Domestic Violence while in Florida. It was almost alarming how many women are abused in America, especially when we're considered a nation of so called laws and such. Honestly, one might get the impression quite easily that no one gives a dam, and truthfully you'd be right. But for all practical purposes let say you're a 37 years old female in fairly good physical condition, intelligent and caring and somewhat attractive. You gotta so so job and not necessarily a beauty queen but truthfully, not bad on the eyes. Let's face it, no man's ever kicked you out of bed at 8:00 am if you know what I mean.

You may not think you have much to offer but don't sell yourself short. The race of love is not about speed but endurance. Many women often feel there biological clock tick, tick, ticking away and feel there constantly running out of time. well I'm here to tell you there's no rush ladies, the gene pool is quite contaminated and will be for quite some time so pick your pools carefully before jumping in. Now these day's between Craig's list providing the latest batch of homicidal maniac's, and other on-line dating sites providing the rest, it's hard to believe anybody's could still be lonely more less alive in America. But really, before you get all Michael Jackson sensitive about everything regarding your on-line dating sites, I think there's a few things that you should know. Did you know that most men on these dating sites have different names on different sites. Oh yeah… many of them even go from site to site searching for the right victim. Oh..sorry about that. I meant to say the right women to spend the rest of there lives with. I know some of you aren't old enough the remember the mail order bride craze like I do. Back in the 80's you could buy a Chinese girl that could clean, have sex and make a mean Egg Foo Young at the same time. The bad part was she was most likely some used up sexual servant being sold by some Chinese Gang to payoff a debt.

Who of course would later be extorted the man she married for money and any tangible property they could get. Those gangs thanks to our American divorce laws bag major bucks…you know, Half of everything which of course provided well for them. Well guess what? Today's is your lucky day, because uncle "P" that's me, is about to school you in the fine art of scum bags 101. I like to poetically call this <u>10 Signs you better run like hell</u>. In this chapter I'm going to tell you about the top 10 scumbag scams used by dead beat daddy's. We'll also discuss infidelity fruit loops, lying low life con men and the biggest creeps on the rise today identity thieves so let's do it. The Top 10 signs you'd better put your Nike's on.

1) You just meet this gorgeous guy and 2
weeks later he ask you for Money.

2) He tells you he's currently between jobs
right now but its temporary because he's
got a buddy that's gonna hook him up later.

3) He arrive's for his first date on a
broken down bicycle, his excuse? he's going
green.

4) He needs to make a phone call and ask
to borrow your phone because his is out of
minutes.

5) When you start to order your food he
cuts you off and he ask, Oh my god are you
gonna eat that!

6) When ever you start a conversation
about you, he cuts you off and start one
about him.

7) He tells you he's was living off of his
 parents trust fund, but his lawyer stole it.

8) He complains about the service at the
restaurant. As well as the food, the waiter,
the waitress, the silverware, the water, the
lights, the music, the heat, The noise..you
get the picture. The sad part is he picked
the restaurant.

9) When you start tell a story about
something he corrects you. And it's not
even his story.

10) His dating profile say's he's a devout
Christian, but he starts the date by
ordering a Jack & Coke. Sweet Jesus!!

<u>Asking for money</u> If you meet a guy, be it on-line or in person and within the first 2 weeks he starts telling you about his tragic life. His mother just died from rabies or he's running short on cash because his cleaning lady robbed him or better yet he just sold a family heirloom and the check bounced......stop!!! Think and use this response" Wow I'm really sorry to hear about your situation, I wish I could help but the my Aids treatments are so expensive. By the way could you be a dear and run me to the clinic tomorrow my cars in the shop. Now when I told this lady to use this excuse 3 years ago she though I was crazy, but then she used it and never heard from the dead beat again. Good thing to seems lover boy had 10 dates scheduled with 10 different women that week alone. She would later learned that 4 of 10 women who went out with him gave him a total of $3000.00. That's one hell of a living ladies think about it, a professional on-line dater could possibly make $12,000.00 a month if he's got a silver tongue and over a $100,000 yearly.

<u>He's currently between jobs</u>- A lot of dead beats will use this ex-cuse if they think they can get a woman to support them. This seems to work well on those lost kitten types. You know the ones,

they love to bring home strays of any variety because they feel as though there doing something good for the world. Well stop, and listen, you're not making a difference, Actually your screwing it up for everybody. So make the date with this guy your last and move on.

He say's he's going green- Now I got nothing against going green but what the f**k does that mean! Well.. any ideas? Well I have a question. Does this mean all your future dates will be driven by rickshaw or will you be wiping you ass with re-cycle pine bark in the future. If that's the case you may wanna see a doctor, for that rash your probably going to have real soon. Better yet are you going meatless too, because I love a woman with a good appetite. And in my opinion there better be some animal protein accompanying that relationship because being honest I hate chick weed.

He has to borrow your cell phone - Really ladies C'mon their like $50 bucks a month, what kinda guy can't afford $50 bucks a month? Oh yeah, one that's incarcerated. I bet when he say's "where going out for dinner" it's not actually a restaurant, but to the bus stop for a bag of potato chips and a Mountain Dew. Please, stop the madness.

<u>Oh my god you're eat that</u>- Ok let me lead with the obvious here, You're a gown ass woman. No wait, You're a free white woman in America, No, No! Better than that, you're a free black woman in America. And while he's sitting there looking stupid trying to tell you what you can and can't eat, tell him to pass the salt and the hot sauce. Let's get something straight you're looking for an equal not a master and this guy has control freak written all over his face. So listen, I know you have no idea what he's doing so I'll tell you, It's a test. He wants to see if he can get you to change your mind to suit his, and if you do it once he'll never stop asking. Remember, you are who you are or as my momma use to say "What you see is what you get". Don't ever pretend your something your not because once the truth is exposed you will always look like nothing but a liar…period.

<u>When ever you start a conversation</u> about you he cuts you off, Ladies this is a sure sign of a man consumed with himself. Don't get involved with a man like this because he's the type of man that needs constant praise or even worse has low self esteem. Guy's like this brag about themselves constantly because somethings missing in their life. The thing is guy's like this always need the spotlight, which of course means your accomplishments will always go un-

recognized. There are always two people within the marriage unless your Mormon, and believe me no woman wants to spend her life being Un-recognized by her man.

Living off of a trust fund- Please….And on a dating website? I know a few trust fund babies and none them have female problems except the drunks, drug addicts and sociopaths. Non of which you should be interested in.

He complains about everything-Let's cut to the chase shall we… can you say asshole! And if your thinking assholeisum is something you out grow out of, I'm happy to disappoint you. There is nothing in this world worse than a male winer, save your Zoloft money and just say no.

He corrects your conversations- Ok, know it all! Nobody wants somebody walking behind them correcting everything they do or say all day long. Forget the Zoloft….Get a GUN!

He starts preaching while drinking a Jack & Coke-Laugh if you want but this is one of the most common things that you'll ever run into on a date, a self righteous drunk. Let me say any kind of chemical dependency is Un-acceptable.

In the end after 20 years of dealing with the lowest forms of society it all comes down to one simple fact. Bullshit artist have one true weapon, those are <u>words</u>. The other weapon they use is within you <u>trust</u>. In law enforcement we refer to these kinds of cases as <u>Device's of Trickery</u>, in other words a man tricking you out of your hard earned money it's not necessarily a crime when you willingly give it to him. You must first be aware that this is the twenty-first century and our politicians and political beliefs have virtually made most cases like this Un-winnable. Therefore we must rely on our own morals to guide us threw these schemes. I would love to tell you that these 10 signs are the only 10 you have to worry about, but I can't because it only goes down hill from here. Older women should pay closer attention to the dating pool especially if you have a significant amount of savings to work with. Young men are far more technologically advance that older women so it's important to protect yourselves and keep up with the latest gadgets. Remember anyone can become a victim at the right place or at the right time so let's go over the closing facts.

*Never co-sign for anything for anyone, if he or she is an adult and got themselves into it, they should work harder to get themselves out of it.

*Never lend money to anyone and if you do always have a written agreement, and if you do have an agreement make sure it conforms with the laws of your state. If you're lending a significant amount of money you should seek the advice of legal counsel for the facts.

*Never give to much information about yourself on the first date, keep your family history to a minimum just in case true love turns into a phishing expedition for personal information.

*Don't be in such a hurry to invite a man to your home, If something goes wrong after your intimate encounter the creep has one up on you already. If he's cool with having sex tell him to pay for the hotel, he should be cool with that if both of you went dutch. If not oh well! Later dude.

* If you're going out on multiple dates don't go to the same places you always go to. There's nothing worse than running into a disgruntle former date when you're out having a good time with someone else. So Get out and see the city just be safe about it.

*Last but not least if you intend to do a lot of drinking I suggest you go out with the girls and not the guy's. It maybe a little safer that way and remember what I said about the drinks, once you walk away from it, dump it an order fresh. Watch out for the druggies.

If you follow these steps there are no guarantees that someone won't try anything but you'll keep them on their toes..good luck

False claims and innuendo's

The great debate…to believe or not to believe

Our society has recently become riddled with false sexual claims and innuendos, the fact is we as Americans have become stagnated with gossip and rumor. But to understand the devastation that false claims and rumors towards people can cause we must first examine the complications of ignoring them. There's an old saying I'm sure many of you may be slightly familiar with, especially older people like me "Believe half of what you hear and part of what you see". We live in a culture dominated by talk shows host that have basically flooded the air waves with gossip of any kind for ratings they can get. And the truth is we as Americans hungrily eat it up. But by watching and listening to these types of negative programs are we setting ourselves up for stereotypes in the future that could bit us all in the ass on day. And if so, what does that mean for us and our futures as Americans. Lets face it, eventually we're all be called to serve in that one place that every American has a god given right to serve...The Courtroom. You would actually be shock to know how many people bring up the Jerry Springer show or some other corn ball example in the jury room when deliberating a case. I myself once had jury duty on a robbery and sexual assault case of a 68 year old woman. In this case a hispanic male broke into her home and believe it or not fell asleep after sexually assaulting this lady. He claimed he was invited over for drinks by the victim except for one small problem…he broke in through the window instead of knocking on the front door. Now I'm willing to hear just about any kind of excuse but the window.. really? Now before you start to pass judgement on this guy you should wait for the entire story to unfold. Now as a man I myself in my younger day's, much much younger day"s have climbed through my share of windows. Maybe for a little more than ahhhh…good night kiss if you know what I mean. And depending on the type of weapons the father had in his possession, I would wait outside or take my chances with getting caught. But there's a difference here.

This was no 16 year old teen and there was no gun toting dad waiting in the living room. This was a plain ole sexual assault. In fact documents in the case file would reveal that he was so intoxicated when he broke into her home that he never bothered to turn the light's on. What's even more disturbing was he actually broke into the wrong trailer, according to him it was another lady he was looking for. The trailer she lived in was 2 trailers down and that lady was actually on vacation. Apparently when the cops arrived he told them had lost his keys at the local bar and decided he would climb in through the window. Now many of you may actually question the rape charge like I did but remember, drunk is drunk and regardless of any chemical influences he was still responsible for his own actions. The interesting part was how many people felt bad for this guy including myself, so much so that it almost hung the jury. Now if your asking how, I'll be more than happy to tell you. It's because most of the jury was composed of young males, most of whom drank on a daily bases. Of course this was a good choice of jurors picked by the Public Defender assigned to the case. The truth was this guy almost walked right out of the courtroom. But thanks to the state Attorney he didn't, if it hadn't been for the State's Attorney's second closing argument well let's just say freedom was in his grasp.

What I'm trying to say is even though he committed a crime there was a lot of us that were willing to let this guy go with a coke and a smile because we felt bad, but that's what jury's do. But something this old lady said kept me thinking, in her testimony she said she heard him coming through her bedroom window and she asked "who's there" and he politely said his name. Oddly enough most burglars wouldn't do that, she then stated in the report that he came in sat down next to her on the bed and they started talking. After roughly 20 mins of small talk the started having sex, wait I'm sorry he forced himself upon her. She did have some bruises but nothing like the kind I've seen on some of the sexual assault victims I know. But yet and still it could have been legit, I don't know I wasn't there. Amazingly enough some of the guy's thought the old lady was some kind of super freak, even some of the women were on the fence with the super freak theory. And honestly, I could think of a half dozen ways to trick a drunk out of a bedroom. Most women know how to do that naturally. But she also claim the guy had a knife, of course by the time the cops got there he was passed out and the knife was on the floor next to the bed. But still it made no sense. Why bring a knife to home you were invited to, where you were supposedly expected. Did he really need protection and if so from what? And lastly she said the sex lasted roughly 5 minutes and then he fell asleep, why wait 15 mins to sneak out and call the cops.

Like I said it made no sense, even more bazar was the 911 call they played. There was no stress at all in her voice, she was as cool as a cucumber. But with all of that to consider it simply came down to one thing for me, she was claiming raped so who do you believe, her or the drunk? For me after deliberation with my co-jurors it was simple..guilty. Now I know many of you may think, what does this have to do with the price of tea in china, but listen. Every time you call the police to report a crime understand there's the good, the bad and the ugly that comes with that call. Remember, everything you say on the phone is public record so don't expect privacy with a 911 call. Here's something else to think about. When I was 21 yrs old my friends and I went to the county fair outside Tampa Florida. There were a few thousand people there and we noticed some people had snuck booze into the place. Some were actually drinking pretty heavy that night which turned pretty exciting later. After a few hours we decided to leave the fair and started the long drive back home. Just ahead of us we noticed the car weaving back and forth in the road. It looked as though the people in the back seat were fighting, suddenly out of the blue the door flew open and a body rolls right out of the car and down into the ditch. As we got closer to the spot where the body landed, we looked down in the ditch and noticed a girl Laying at the bottom. From where we were standing she looked like she couldn't have been more that 16. As I started to climb down to help the girl my friend yelled out to me "Are you crazy"? He went on to say "You touch that white girl and you'll do 20 years". Now that may have seemed harmless enough to me, but honestly he did have a valid point. See no one saw the car that dumped the girls body ahead of us but us. And because we were the only car behind them, the other drivers had there view blocked by our vehicle. So instead of a rescue attempt we waited for the next car to come by. Needless to say it wasn't long these 3 white guy's that pulled up in the car behind us, we flagged them down and asked For help. One of them walked over to us and looked down and saw the girl laying in the bottom of the ditch and said "Fuck that dude, I ain't touching that bitch". He then jumped back into his car and hauled ass out of there like he just saw an alien. Finally, after what seem like an eternity a nurse drove by with her husband and she asked what's up, when we explained what happen she got out of her car look down and said "for god sake help her". Her husband got out of the car and together we all helped the young lady out of the ditch and up to the side of the road. We told them some guy's tossed her out of a car and she landed in a ditch. The nurse's husband called for help and soon the ambulance arrived which of course was our Que to leave. Oddly enough the next day with all those people driving by it's was incredible to discover that no on actually saw the car that dumped the girls body. But interesting enough if you can believe it, everyone in the county could remember seeing 3 black guy's standing over this white girl's body. This became the narrative for the cop's who arrived on the seen after we left. Now suddenly everyone's looking for 3 black suspects, all because we stopped to help. As African Americans we must never lose track of the fact that there are opportunist everywhere. I would issue a stern warning to any minority to think strongly before rendering assistance to anyone, especially giving deep thought to helping a woman or a man with any kind of head injury or possible drug or alcohol overdose. Even calling 911 could land you in jail depending the town, place and the witnesses involved, especially when the possibility of memory loss may be a concern with the victim. Truly it was a bad decision, it was just plain stupid for us to stop at all. I was only visiting with friends but the driver of the vehicle was good friend of mine. My understanding from him was people would regularly drive by his house yelling crazy things out the window for weeks afterwards. One of the girls family members kept questioning him not to mention following him for weeks, her family even went to his employer and started asking questions. Luckily for us the nurse kept her story straight for the cops. It's not everyday that people feel it necessary do the right thing for others, but we should all be careful not to place ourselves into bad situations. Being in the wrong place at the wrong time could change your life for ever. As for the nurse and her high moral character, we are and forever will be grateful. For most women simply reporting a crime is just the beginning, the fact remains for most victims that's the easy part. What comes next is the dreadful part.

When it comes down to sexual assaults You can consider any and every part of your claim to be suspect until the police have proven of your allegation. This is called the investigative portion of your case, and some of you may find this part more difficult the the actual assault itself. Mainly because it involves long periods of waiting, and lots of questions some of which you'd never expect. At the end of the day the fact remains that the more brutal the assault the more questions people will ask, not just about the suspect but about the victim too. You should never be surprised when you're suddenly labeled a lying, cheating, bi-polar sex addict by the family of the accused, and you should expect some type of blow back. They'll always say that your blaming an innocent man for your twisted sexual fantasy, one that you yourself created. The truth is, most married women never report 75% of there Sexual Assaults by anyone. Mainly again because of the embarrassment of facing the accused in court as well as the media in public. This often creates a difficult situation for the police investigating the crime while at the same time creating reasonable doubt for the defense. Most married women who were sexually assaulted would rather hide and denied the rape or assault happen that actually say it did. And as strange as this may sound, most women have complained of the same basic problems after reporting the crime:

1) Fear that there husbands would never
Understand. Many actually blame their wives.

2) Fear that there husbands would reject
 them afterwards. Many women have gone on the say
there husbands never touch them again.

3) The stigmata associated with the public
scrutiny of a sexual assault. People will talk, whisper
And make up things about you. Sorry ladies nothing
you can do about that.

All of which I feel are senseless and totally unnecessary for such a awful crime. For a long time in the late 80's and early 90's we had a lot of victim assistance programs sponsored by the federal government, many of these programs would assist victims of sexual assault crimes with there recovery. But now that our political climate has change, many such victims are basically consider expenditures within our society. They no longer consider a victim worthy of services, and no longer see victim services as a problem for the government. But If you are a victim of sexual assault there are still places that you can go for help while maintaining your anonymity. You should research this careful before holding this terrible crime inside and hiding from what you've experienced. But if and when you do find the courage and the heart to stand up and report your crime, you need to know what to expect. These are some of the most effective defenses for any Sexual assault:

Consensual sex- The violent nature of the sex was not abuse, it was basically your idea and involved role play, and was orchestrated solely and completely by you. You shouldn't be surprised if the accused claims that the two of you had sex on a previous occasion, just to muddy the waters. Truth is it's worked before but not often, this is mostly done when a lot of men are on the jury, but you shouldn't be concerned because changing the narrative is done quite often.

The victim not only enjoyed it but she had an orgasm- It can't be rape if the victim has and orgasm. Some of you may have heard this Ugly piece of scientific bullcrap in the 2010 elections. Even though it was total garbage it did gain some traction among conservatives, You should be warned that a Defense Attorney could throw this at you while your on the stand. But first, you must understand that this is a natural response to physical stimulus. I have spoken to well over 120 women of domestic and sexual violence and I would say at least 30% or more of them have had some type of orgasm depending on the type of assault and the amount of violence during the attack. It has even happen to some men while being sexually assaulted while in Jail or in Prison. And it becomes a psychological nightmare if it happens, one most men and women can never live down. This is the shameful part of sexual assaults especially for a man or woman that's married. This is why married men and women often hold back details that later comeback to bit them in the ass. And in my opinion they should, if you are aa victim of a sexual assault and this does happen to you never, I mean never, speak of it again! Tell know one because this could undermine your entire case. Remember what I said earlier, 12 people who know <u>absolutely nothing about</u>.

<u>Mistaken Identity</u>- induced by Drug, alcohol or some type of chemical influence or mental defect. It's a lot harder to prove sexual assault when you've been under the influence of something. Defense Attorney's usually have a field day with this especially with the identification part and the part of consent. They'll usually question your memory or your clarity of the previous nights events. You should also keep most of the fact's between yourself

and your attorney, never vent to others. Talking to Friends could comeback and bit you in the ass or better yet may make it appear as though your lying or you purposely left something out of the story.

Revenge - The victim alleges the crime took place for the purpose of financial or political Gain, or out of retaliation for a previous circumstance. For some strange reason victims are always shock when a criminal suspect lies, Come on ladies only a complete and utter scum bag would rape a woman in the first place. You should be prepared for anything fowl to come from the mouth of the accused. This is one of the main reasons it so hard for women to get on the stand and testify. You not only have to defend your honor an integrity but any un-substantiated claims as well. But be careful, don't get sucked into a tip for tap with the accuse's Defense Attorney while on the stand. Truth is, if your not planning on to taking the stand during the trial don't even waste your time with filing the charges. Everyone will question weather or not your lying or not. I'm not saying it's going to be easy but I want you to know the risk your taking when you expose yourself to 12 people who know positively nothing about you. At the same time you must realize if you say nothing and do nothing this guy will go on and on and on. His violence will more than like escalate as he builds more confidence on the fact that no one's reporting his crimes. That's why they often pick married women in the first place. He knows the odds are in his favor. These are very effective defensive claims, not because they make sense, but because most single guy's on a jury can relate. Remember they don't know what happen to you unless you tell them. I'm shocked as a bondsman how many times guy's will beat these charges in open court, there's always a jailhouse lawyer around to advise the criminal, but never one for the victims. When stepping forward to report your sexual assault you must consider all the possibilities. Like, Can you truly identify your assaulter, or were you drinking or were you drunk, and did you use any recreational drugs that night. If you got high with your accuser, your going to have a tough road ahead. Did you know him personally or prior to the assault, and if so what was the nature of your relationship. You should expect every dirty trick in the book and nothing should surprise you. But most of all, when you report your crime to the police you should never use the words "I'm not sure or could be or I think so". These words tell the police that you can't positively identify your attacker, and no one wants to put the wrong person in jail and neither should you. However, if there is any DNA that could possibly be to your advantage, you should allow the police to collect as much as possible. In the real world these procedures must take place to get the bad guy's off the street.

Domestic Violence

The fight for life What is Domestic violence

We're all familiar with the Hollywood version of domestic violence on our televisions, but the truth is the real life versions is a hell of a lot worse and twice as scary. The real life version will always be far worse than any motion picture can ever betrays it because it's <u>real</u>. Real blood, real wounds and real broken bones and real pain, not to mention the real emotional wreckage left behind. So we'll start with some examples of true domestic violence so you'll understand.

Example 1

True story!!!

I was contacted as a Bondsman by a woman in the Great State of Alabama to assist with providing bail for her boy friend of several years. As I begin to discuss the process of bail and what's normally required to secure my services, I often ask what happened. This normally gives you and idea weather or not you want to get involved with the client or past the buck so to speak. During my conversation with the client I notice a change in her voice. I ask the young lady "Are you alright". She then stated "yes but it's my last little bit of money". Now being a Bondsman we've heard it all before. Really, I mean it! We have literally heard every excuse there is when it comes time to pay your bail money and remove some-one from Jail. And amazingly enough while listening to this lady I'm starting to feeling that strange sensation right now. I'm starting to think to myself "Here comes another one, get ready". But for some reason this one sounded a little different. Seems she's been with this guy for over 3 years and the relationship has been volatile since it's conception. But for some reason this time he took it to a whole new level. First he took a metal clothes hanger and heated over a gas stove until it glowed red, then he made her strip off he pants and he began beating her without mercy between her legs. As she continued with the gory details I thought to myself "what the hell".

As she went on with the details of her brutal assault, she men-tion needing close to 15 stitches in her private part's to stop the bleeding. The doctor also told her she would need several skin graph surgery's to fix the damage the red hot hanger left behind. Now most Bondsman have one simple rule, never ask questions or get involved and above all, Never ask a question you don't want to know the answer to. Why? Prosecutors and Defense Attorney's that's why. They will subpoena you to the courtroom in a heart-beat if they think you heard them confession to something. In fact anything that would help nail a scumbag or help the defense in anyway could be fair game. Problem is, once people start to hear your turning tricks for the cops (Giving up information on your clients) your on a slow boat to being out of business. Anyway, back to the story. So, I committed the cardinal sin when I asked. "Why in the world would you stay with someone like that. What possible purpose would it serve to continue living with them". She turned to me and said something I never thought about, "After so many attempts of trying to leave you learn it's safer to stay". It's amazing how fast people can find you in a small town she said, the people you think are your friends really aren't. Every time he caught up with her after she left the beatings got meaner, angrier, and more spiteful. He always convinces me that it was my fault, you don't know how many times I prayed for God to take my life but he wouldn't. Right then it hit me hard, so I asked "you got any kids" she said "yes 2 boys and a girl". I then ask how do you allow some-one to do these things to you in front of your children. I mean doesn't he have any pride. The thing is I actually answered my own question without realizing it. Pride is not a word in the vo-cabulary of a wife beater. But how do women get to this point, and what are the signs that your relationship may be heading forward in this direction. Men of domestic violence are often creatures of habit, The first thing a woman should notice is there absence of value. Absence of value simply means a man no longer see's your worth or asset to the relationship. See, when you first start a relationship with a man you typically provide that man with something special, you provide him with comfort, spiritual support, assurance and for many women financial support. These thing's create a sense of value in a relationship for any woman that no one can put a price on, but when a man start's beating you or cheating on you, you no longer have value with that man. I use to wonder often why men would walk around town with a woman battered bruised standing next to them, for me it seem degrading. And the more I thought about it the more I realized I couldn't do it myself. Someone who looked like that with those type's of injuries, you'd want to keep as far away from you as possible. Most of the time, wife beaters and domestic abusers will follow the same behavior patterns. Possessive with explosive temper's, very insecure and highly argumentative, and most must have complete control of every situation as well as the victim at all times. For them it's not about the relationship, it's about controlling and belittling at every opportunity. A true domestic abuser will never pass up a chance to take a shot at his victim anywhere anytime, be it physical or mental. This is the compulsion part of there behavior, the part where they intend to emphasize total control over not only over the situation but the very being themselves. Remember domestic violence is not just physical, it can be mental too, and one should never forget the mind is a fragile piece of equipment. Domestic abusers take great pride in disassembling there victims souls, remember a rape is never about sex it's about control. It's about letting a bitch know who's boss and making sure she never forgets it. Some traits of possible Domestic Abuser will alway's show themselves in the early stages of any dating relationship:

1) Sudden mood swings - He may be calm now and suddenly explode with rage, one possible sign is if someone else upsets him and he will naturally finds a way to blame you.

2) Hyper possessive tendencies - Women involved with Men in these types of relationships aren't considered people but property. Remember he'll treat you like nothing more than another possession, no different than a watch or a car.

3) The Challenge - They despise being

challenged by anyone, especially women.
When they speak about women it's sounds
sometimes like a distant hatred of
sorts. Sometime's referring to you the
spouse in the third person, I never got that one.

4) Woman are Always Wrong - They will
often go through great pains to prove to a
Woman that there wrong. They will argue
for hours until you give up or get the point,
and will often raise there voice's when you
stand your ground. This is and
Intimidation tactic, funny thing in the
prison system there all as quiet as church
mouse's. That may have something to do
With being in a room full of true killer's.
You know what they always say, silence is
 golden.

5) Men are Insecure - There very insecure
And for some strange reason a fair
Percentage of them often have erectile

dysfunction, something I also learned from the prison psychiatric nurse. There very Easily intimidated sexually, which can causes them to lash out.

6) Never Satisfied - They're never satisfied, no matter what you do, the satisfaction is always temporary. Even if you do everything just the way they like it, they'll never compliment on your good deeds.

7) Woman are not to be in the Spotlight- They will never, I mean never, allow you to Have your day in the spotlight. They'll often try everything in there power to ruin Your big day. If the day is all about you they'll always try to instantly deflate the moment.

8) The Word "No" - If you're dating one of these men and ask for space they'll often become agitated, Possible Domestic

Violence abusers hate the word "No". Any time you suggest something it will alway's sounds stupid or dumb or make no sense to him. It's the subtle insults that make the moment obvious.

Now let's talk what if, what happens if you realize that the guy of your dreams turns out to be some sort of society Misfit. If your first two dates were great only to have the third become the date from hell, what do you do. First remember all scumbags leaves a residue. Yes, all of them, and like all residue's it may take time to get rid of it. Just because your dating day's are over doesn't mean that your rejected former boyfriend will just go gently into the night. Nooo. I've got some nightmare stories to share, but I shouldn't. Why? Well you'd probably never date again, never. But the next time you catch me in your city ask me one on one I'll be happy to tell you. Anyway, if you find yourself being romantically pursued by a Psychopath, you must start laying the foundation for a Stalker Defense. Whether your married or not you have the right to live in peace. If you met this guy on-line he will more than likely have sent you some type of Trojan Horse Virus to track your every move while on your computer. You should also be aware that some court's typically don't recognize a stalking defense for married women. Once you get a legal separation or just plain ole separate that's a different story and this is where the fun start's. One of the hardest things I've ever understand is when a man beats a women in a dysfunctional relationship, or watching him try to kill her if she attempt's to leave. Surely you would think since the relationship was tanking, all's well that end's well right? Wrong, These guy's will often go for blood, the ole saying "If I can't have you no one can" will always comes into play. Remember what I told you earlier, These guy's work hard to make your life a living hell, and thats the joy of terror for a terrorist. To them, your not just property your an investment, think of it this way. The about the amount of time he spent making your life totally miserable, screaming, yelling, insulting and smacking you around, are you serious you want to leave? Hell no! It took him 5 years to ruin your life, knock your teeth out and crack you ribs, how dare you leave, he's not done yet. He can't allow that, that means he has to start all over again with someone else. And we all know once you break up with somebody you've trained like a dog for 5 years it's never the same, no one wants to start over again from scratch. True story listen. A woman married to a guy for 10 years in a abusive relationship finally gets the courage to leave. So on the night the judge grants her a initial separation she goes out with friends to celebrate. After there meal they all prepare to leave the restaurant together and go to a local night club when the husband suddenly pulls up behind her. He jumps out of his pickup truck, pulls her out of the car by her hair, and literally kicks her unconscious. After doing so gets back into his pickup truck and flee's the seen. When the wife get's to the hospital she can't remember anything that happened because of the head trauma, but here's the sick part. She has a broken jaw, 5 broken ribs, a broken arm and massive head trauma. But wait it gets even better, while she's in the hospital unconscious on her death bed the husband and has his lawyer cook up a scheme and file for custody of the children, stating how she was unfit medically. The judge not realizing that the reason that she's unfit, was because her husband beat her unconscious in the parking lot, grant's the order to the husband. The husband while the wife's still in the hospital sells there home and her car to pay for his possible legal defense and move's out of state. And after about 5 week stay in the hospital she comes home to find she has no longer has a home, or car and no kids. And on top of all this madness there's no sign of her husband anywhere. And thats the good news, now here's the bad news. Being those good Southern conservative folks they are of this small town, all those witnesses that were there decide not to get involved in the situation. So not only was she beaten to a bloody pulp, loss her house, her car and kids, her husband got away Scott free with attempted murder. You see, because no one would testify against the husband he was able to make up his own version of what happen and call it self defense. See everybody in town knew he had a few screws loose, but nobody wanted him coming back to attack them so he got away with the crime. In the end, the system failed this women as it often as it does many of us. The difference for us is this, do you go out fighting or begging on your knees. The difference between a law abiding citizen and a criminal is often not morality, it's fear. Fear of the unknown, the fear of loss, your house, your family, your freedom. Fear is a powerful motivator of circumstance's, but above all fear changes the consequences of our actions. Criminals don't have this fear, it's partially the reason they continue there constant cycle of criminal activity and the consistent cycle of and going in and out of jail. When you begin to lose fear of something, you'll eventually lose respect for it, which is why most criminals have no respect for themselves as well as the system. Your job ladies if you choose to except it is simple, to find a man that loves you for you. I know this may seem like a tall request but remember good thing's take time. All beautiful things that grow on god's green earth took millennia to create. Which is why seeing them bloom make's it all so sweet and worth while. I would like to see all of you in healthy relationships, but that my friends is nothing more than a dream. You will run into the occasional scumbag, misfit and reject everyday of your live's, but that's what make's finding the right one so important. See you all in volume 2.

Sexual Deviants and

The skin trade

Pimps, Child Molesters and Pedophile's

First question, what is the skin trade? The skin trade is the street name for Prostitution and Human Trafficking. This will probably be one of the most important chapters that you will have to study for this book so please pay attention. The importance of this chapter is self explanatory for several reasons:

1) Sexual definitions and descriptions

2) Popular schemes

3) Hunting Grounds

4) Recruitment tactics

Sexual Definitions commonly used on the street:

Bull Queer - A known homosexual who has a dominate nature. There are two types of bull queers most are rather violent by

nature with quick tempers the other type
simply refers to the method of the lifestyle
they live. The man of the relationship
basically. Most bull queers in the prison
system must never be taken lightly because
of there explosive tempers.

Closet Queer - A homosexual who prefers
to keep his sexual activities in the closet so
to speak. This type of inmate/person will be a
straight male using sexual favors for the
simple purpose of survival. Or sneaking out at
night for personal pleasure

May-tag - Straight guy turn within a
homosexual slave by the system usually by
a particular person or gang. May be bought
And sold at random from gang member to
gang member, many will have to pay due's
or percentages depending on where they're
housed within the unit.

<u>Pedophiles</u> - A type of sexual deviant that prefers have sex with minors typically 8 years and older. It is often said that pedophiles mostly prefer boy's but my experience is that's not true. Sexual deviants have the ability to adapt to many different circumstance. The main differences that I've observed is that pedophiles actually have a warped sense of love for children, they believe there true love for a child is genuine. The truth about about these guy's is as long as the child doesn't have pubic hair and haven't gone through puberty yet there all fair game. The love these people feel for children is often an over whelming thing. It's said that pedophiles have The most sophisticated network of communications in the world because most are highly, highly educated.

<u>Chicken Hawks</u> - Another form of pedophile but typically 40+ that only has sex with

minor boy's. Chicken hawks though rare
have been known to have sex with boy's as old
as 25 years of age

<u>Child Molester</u> - There are many
definitions for this term but all you need
to know is this. This is a compulsion that
can't be helped by some really confused
guy's. They're experts at be friending
children by either gift or favor I.e. Candy,
toys, small animals working on or fixing
bicycles, toys, or other things of value for
children. They can sometimes be recognized
by the gift's they give. Remember child
molesters typically have an ugly nature
towards children which is
common for this type of deviant. Usually
bought on if the child threatens to reveal
their identity or no longer wants to
participate in there sexual activities. One
note to moms, the child molester I've seen
are methodical in nature and true child

molesters are very disciplined and can hide in plain site. There are some signs though, once they find a child there interested in there like a lion watching pray very focused. And most, can't stop fantasizing and must make contact with there victim, so beware.

Shrums - The latest craze for pedophiles is paying runaways and local bullies to recruit kids for them. This works very well Because there's no shortage of angry kids looking to exploit other children for a dollar. The old saying "are you a big kid or what" really works. If you were to ask 20 children between the ages of 4 and 5 about there age they would all tell you they're 4 and a half. That compulsion to be a big kid is so over whelming that most would do anything they're asked to prove there big. Most of the time you don't have to abducted a child, just have another child

convince them to follow a long and this is not
 a crime so to speak. The plan is
to convince a child that he or she is big
enough to do what the other kids do.
Because there children, police have no
grounds to actually suspect fowl play or a
possible kidnapping in progress. For a
teenager working for a known Pedophile or
Child Molester it's strictly about the
money. This practice became big primarily
in the 90's due to our society placing huge
emphasis on money above all things.
Children are far easier to convince around
a crowds of other children to do something
than when they're by themselves mainly do
 to pier pressure.

But for the moment let's continue with the definitions we have
due basically because they happen to be the most popular group
of deviants in America right now. In the early 80's there were a lot
of sexual deviants living among us, many of them right under most

of our nose's and many of you never knew it. The fact is sexual deviants have been interacting with normal society for well over 1000 years and there masters at blending in. Most are well respected members of the community that go to church, attend P.T.A meetings and even volunteer at bake sale's and civic functions. In fact, I had one inmate in my custody serving a 10 year sentence for sexual assault of a minor who actually formed his own Boy Scout troop. Yes people, the fox was guarding the hen house. Another was posing as a church Paster for more than 10 years right under the congregations nose. He was counseling alter boy's privately for years if you know what I mean, before some of the boy's started coming forward.

Some of the first forms of social deviance was known as sexual slavery, which has been documented as far back as the ancient Greeks. Back then, rich wealthy notable men would use children as payment when collecting debts owed by there parents. In fact these servant house's were some of the first known house's of I'll repute, where both boy's and girl's were placed in to sexual servitude. Fast forward to today, the names's may have change but the people remain the same. The problem is the game has changed a lot. What you should know is that these people are intelligent and well organized and heavily, I mean heavily funded by sources from all over the world. Next to Drug dealing, Child porn is one of the highest forms of revenue in the world and it's possible that in the future it could over take the drug game by billions. Child pornography is cheap and easy because most children come from foreign countries, where unfortunately there are very few laws in place to protect them. In fact the primary source for most of these kids is South America and Asia because of the gripping poverty in some of these societies. Most of the time people in poor third world countries can't afford birth control, so if they have to many children some may resort to desperate measures. As sad as it may be, it is a well known fact that some sacrifice's may hurt far more than others.

And no matter the situation I myself could never do something so desperate to my child. Some of the most dangerous sexual predators are the most creative in nature. I remember when I was seven years old an old man offer me a Mary Jane. For those of you who aren't old enough to know what that is, it's the name of a variety of candy. I remember him distinctly telling me to reach into his pocket and pull out the candy, needless to say there was more in his pocket than just candy. But even at seven I could sense there was something wrong with this picture, even I knew something was off. Ladies, when I speak about these thing's it's not from text books for me, it's been part of my real life. I remember asking him "what is that" and him telling me "pull on it and see, pull it, go ahead pull harder". As I would think about it years later, and it would occur to me 17 years after attending the academy that I was the victim of one of the oldest pedophile ticks in the book, baiting with candy. Thinking about it, we as children love things like candy, balloons, puppy's, kittens, birds and everything else that fascinates us as children. Even as adults we are often fascinated by things we don't understand or find interesting to the eye, so how in the world would a child ever stand a chance. I use to talk to my littlest sister about my experience until she told me "Just get over it, stop using it as a crutch for god sake and man up, stop blaming mom for your problems".

Now interesting enough the reason I was put in that situation was because my mom was actually sneaking off and having an affair with a married man. Apparently, she was desperate to find a baby sitter for a last minute rendezvous. And in so doing, she was willing to dropped me off at the home of the neighborhood pedophile, lucky me. It would be seventeen years later as an officer in the Department of Corrections that I would actually run into my actual sexual attacker. Yes people, face to face with the man himself, but with one major difference, he was now a very old and fragile man. He was also now a very sick man with Aids. His file would reveal he had a history of attacking children and now with Aids, took great pride in spreading the virus to his young victims. I would leave may shift that night and return home to confide in the one person in the world that I could always confide in, my wife. I learned one important lesson early on in life. Never confide in your siblings about such delicate matters less you risk being labeled the family misfit. To this day I blame myself which is why it was so important for me to write this book. Truth is, if you can't talk about it, then write about it. The choice to publish your writings are strictly up to you. The Department of Corrections was a learning ground for me, what I saw there would be my inspiration for this book, but also for me personally.

See, running into my attacker as a officer was a tough experience for me both physically and mentally. So when I was able to assist women at a local shelter who had been attacked by others I kinda had an idea what they were going through. Minus of course the brutal beatings. One of the things I've always found fascinating about sexual predators was the spirit of where there's a will theres a way. I'd never seen someone Masturbate in public until my employment in the Department. There you learn and see all the tricks of the trade by some of the mort creative Deviants in the world.

like something the inmates poetically called Jacky Jack. This believe or not was a string tied to your big toe with a rubber band wrapped around your penis. The string went from the toe underneath your pants all the way up to the penis, usually with some type of plastic that was moisten with some kind of lubricate. When the inmate wanted to masturbate he simple put his walkman headphones on and pretended to listen to music. Meanwhile, he would tap his foot to the rhythm to conduct the process. The tapping of the foot created a jerking motion on the penis allowing the individual to masturbate without ever touching himself.

This was and still is a well known tactic for pedophile's on play grounds because a public display would immediately bring the cops. You would often see inmates tapping there feet even when there was no music depending on then deviant. On way to ensure wether are not they weren't whacking off was to ask "what are you listen to" most people when listening to music would tell you, Jazz or Hip Hop or top 40. Most will even go into the artist and the song there listening to, but not a <u>Patty Whacker.</u> Patty whackers will say something like "Oh it's a new tune" or my favorite was alway's "Praise Jesus, Gospel Music Sir". Yeah right... sure thing buddy, my response would always be the same "Stop whacking off to the Female Officers, and the male ones too, or You'll go blind". Sad part was a lot of them already wore coke bottle glasses, so what difference would it make. Between that and the ole hole in your pocket trick it was pretty crazy on the yard. I mean some guy's never took there hands out of there pocket's…ever! I hope your paying attention because I'm not telling you this for my health there is a purpose. I will often go to parks to this day and still see the same old tricks used by these guy's especially on restaurant play grounds at fast food places like Mc Donald's. There something about someone sitting on a playground without kids or grand kids all by themselves just watching children. Not to say every person sitting on a playground without a child is a sexual deviant, but they do deserve a second look on occasion if you know what I mean.

You should also be mindful of child stimulants like animals and balloons and other stuff like that, and they love to sit near food trucks and food courts. Food trucks and courts provide perfect cover for watching so be observant, not necessarily of them but of your own children. Part of the problem is most of you are looking so hard for perv's your not paying attention to your own children. The best defense has alway's been a good offense and you, your children will always be naturally curious but it's up to you to protect them. Hunting grounds will alway's change but the agenda for deviants won't, sexual deviant's will alway's adapt to counter measures so you have to stay on your toes. Using children for recruitment purposes is just one way of adapting to modern times within this criminal enterprise. What could be easier for a school yard bully than getting rid of kids you don't like and getting paid to do it. We have to explain to our children that not every child is your friend and to always ask you first before leaving with anyone. Strangely, for some strange reason a lot of parents think staying away from minority children is the key. What the hell? You believe your child is more likely to run off with some minority person than his or her own race.

That's pure ignorance. They're 5 times more likely to run off with there own kind, in fact it's often a very successful recruitment tactic by bullies. So teach your kids that anybody could do harm to them and to never leave with, wonder off with or blindly trust any strangers. I'm sure there's a lot of white parent's out there who wish Ted Bundy hadn't snatched there daughters off the road and chopped them up into little pieces. Truth is he didn't care what color they were, if you caught his attention you were probably the next victim on the list. Race played no part in the equation, he was an equal opportunity serial killer, plain and simple. This is nothing more the a Right Wing tactic to convince you that your safer with one race than the other. The truth is anybody and I mean anybody can hurt you at any time. And don't think prison changes anyone, most of the time it only allows a convicted felon to ponder the mistake's he or she made. Like everything else, we learn from our mistakes, take for example Jeffery Dahmer. When one of Dahmers victims got away, a 14-year-old Laotian boy who was seen running naked down the street past the home of his african american neighbor, who then saw the boy and called the police. Some how he as a white person, was able to convince the police that a 14 year old boy frantically running down the street naked was actually his 19 year old lover.

Dahmer told the police that they were lovers and the kid was on drugs and they had a disagreement, and the police bought it. Not just bought it, but gave them both a ride back to Dahmer's home… together. Against the strong protest of one of Dahmers neighbor's who clearly saw the kid was completely terrified, the police agreed to leave the kid with Dahmer. But before doing so the police walked inside the home, looked around, turned around and left. Here's the thing, just in the other room 20 feet away, was his twelfth victims decomposing body. In most police academies recruits are often taken to the Medical Examiners office so they can familiarize themselves with that smell. This is one of the most important trips you can ever give a recruit, to smell that smell is to never forget it. The question is, how did those officers miss that smell, I mean no amount of febreeze can cover that smell up, that's a very distinctive smell. Which brings me to our next subject Runaways. It's believed that most kids runaway from home simply because they can't get what they want from there parents. Sometimes this is true but more than likely there's more going on than meets the eye. Roughly about 30% of the time there's some type of abuse going on inside the household, but rarely do we as citizen choose to intervene. A dysfunctional family is the main prerequisite for Pimps and Gang Bangers, they use this in there recruitment tactics for gaining trust over weak mined teens. If a young underage girl leaves home abruptly, within the first 48 hours she will discover she needs one thing above all…protection. These streets have no mercy for anyone, man, woman, or child. When a girl is first approached by a pimp the pimps main concern or objective is not her safety, but to keep her from rival pimps. There is a special market for younger girls, in fact, as soon as they hit the street the price for these young girl's can be 3 times that of a woman over 20 years of age. The first move for a pimp is typically to drug the young girl, this is especially important if she is in fact a virgin. The second move is to relocate the girl away from her home area, that being if anyone should spot the girl on the street, no one would recognize her. This will usually be done in some off the wall town in some roach motel some where off the beaten path. Criminals tend to use the same motels basically because those that take cash ask no questions. The process of drugging usually will numb the pain of sexual intercourse for the first time. Pimps will normally not hit these younger girls because leaving any marks or bruises will alway's lower the value of the product. Because she's a virgin most pimps will have a client list of John's who prefer these types of girls, but they don't want to deal with the screaming and crying. Well, not all, some John's do like that kind of sickness. Once a client has done his business she's fair game for the first level freaks. These are the guy's who don't necessarily want virgins but do like them young. Remember, any girl under 15 years of age will command top dollar especially to foreign perv's and specialized clients. Depending on the family and the connections the pimp poses, she could be shipped off to just about anywhere. But sooner or later the pimp will stop drugging the girl, why, because it's time for her to wake up and smell the coffee. This is where pimp psychology 101 come's into play, the pimps job is a simple one. The pimp must convince the girl that he and himself is her one and only best friend. Remember young girl's with bruises make less money. This, is to be done strictly by skill, and some of the pimp's that I know are some real smooth talkers. The game is simple, let her know her family has abandon her, he might say "hell they haven't even sent anybody out to look for you girl". This plays well into the theme of why she left home in the first place, the feeling of being un-loved and un-wanted is powerful thing. What's even worse is as the pimp get's to know her, he may discovers that she was actually being sexually abused at home. This plays directly in favor of the pimp, if she's being force to have sex at home, why not get paid to do it on the streets. This is where the actual kidnapping slowly turns into a relationship situation and the girl eventually accepts her fate. The whole process could take as much as 3 weeks for young girls but a lot less for older one's. People should also remember when a runaway's girl becomes a liability, they have to go, and I don't mean home. However, some girls may actually earn there freedom, I have seen it, but it's rare. I would often hear female inmates layout the whole game and how it works, but I could never understand it myself. If you were forced into life of sexual servitude, why is it the first chance you had to run you didn't. I mean unless you were actually locked into a hotel room and chained to the bed for the last 6 months what kept you there. Every girl I ever asked that question to has said the same thing,"where would I go" and after seeing the things I've seen I believe them. To many of these girls are considered totally disposable and that's not all. First you have to figure out what state your in if you've been moved, some of these girl's have been moved well over 600 miles. Top that off with a 8 day's binder locked in some motel room doped up to the max and anybody would lose track of time and place. Secondly, you ran away from home for a reason, if you were being abused why in god's name would you go back. Some girl's say they would rather die on the streets than go back home and live in a situation like that. Lastly, some of these guy's are beast, just in case you weren't paying attention. You do remember that part about the girl and the pimp talking. Yeah! there's a good chance she probably told the pimp everything he needed to know about her life story. This does not in any way apply to women of age doing this trade by choice, only runaway girls. So in the end it's not all choice for these underage girls, sometimes it just there way of surviving a really bad situation. So the next time you see one of these young ladies standing on the street corner, instead of asking "How Much" Try asking what gives? And are you in trouble, are you safe and do you need help. If so call the cops If you can, but if not, feel better knowing that it's there choice not someone else's.

STALKING

Knowing the difference and how to respond

When you talk about stalking to most people they all seem to have their own Hollywood perceptions of what they think stalking should be. That is, someone standing outside your home in the middle of the night dressed in all black watching your every move through your bedroom window. Well, contrary to popular belief that's not actually stalking, that my friend is a peeping tom. Some-one who gets his kicks looking through windows and peep holes for there personal entertainment or satisfaction. There are a many of peeps out there hiding in bushes nightly in America in hope's of getting a glimpse of someone's panties. What I'm talking about is the genuine article, anonymous flowers left at your door, candy from that perfect stranger, love notes on your desk with no name of sender, you know what I'm talking about. All that good old fash-ion creepy stuff that leaves you paranoid to the point that you can't sleep. Well, just like every other type of criminal behavior stalkers also have there own various traits exclusive to each perv, which we'll discuss later in this chapter, but for now let's move on. I'm sure we all remember back in the day when we all had a secret admirer, I mean for most of us it was quite exciting to think that there was someone out there that had a thing for us. Especially when secretly we had a thing for someone else at the same time. The great hope for most of us was that the person you had a crush on, was the same person that had the crush on us. And all though most of the time it wasn't, every now and then you could get lucky. Well, snap back to reality, in today's society it's not the fact of being the wrong guy or girl you have to worry about more or less, it's what happens when you tell them no. It's the rejection that seems to bring out the nasty bits in most people, especially when it comes to love. Nowadays, many of you are worried more about your image and less about you safety. Honestly it seems that none of you are concern enough to care what may be coming around the corner later on.

In this day and age people have become very unforgiving in situations of the heart, and if your not careful you just might create your very own stalker situation, and here's how. When a person sends you something let's say anonymously, not telling you who it's from, is a sign that they have a fear rejection. After all, who wants to date someone who's afraid to write there name on the back of a card. Honestly, I mean who does that, oh yeah, I know who...stalkers that's who. On the other hand, what's worse than that is writing down a bogus name or someone else's name just to see the your reaction on your face, that's just plain ole mean. Remember, nightmares come in all shapes and sizes and this is not a class on psychology but on survival. At the same time being to nice about the situation could create just as deadly of situation as being to mean about it, could you really say if a person is or isn't a psycho. Depending on the mental stability of any person that your dealing with, you might want to tread lightly. Remember, you are more likely dealing with a fragile and delicate personality here, someone who has been rejected numerous times and fears being rejected again. So, you might want to consider 5 basic things before you decide on cutting loose with a full verbal assault of "Are you f**kin crazy" or "not on your life assh**e" or the ever so popular these day "Get the f**k away from me" line. Truly!

1) <u>Ask the person why they feel attracted</u>

<u>to you</u> - Most of the time it's something
You said positive to a person who was
going through a hard or difficult time in there
live's and the simple fact is your kindness
was completely miss interpreted. This
happens a lot more than you think, so go easy
at first until you find out more.

2) <u>Ask the person what gave them the impression</u>
<u>that you were interested in them</u>- Before you start yelling and

screaming and making a scene. Establish
that in your haste to be friendly or helpful
that you didn't use the wrong wording or
imply something else

3) <u>Analyze the situation as a possible
threat</u>- The reason your talking to this
person is to establish if this is an actual
stalking situation and not just a
case of puppy love.

4) <u>If identified as a potentially hostile don't
over react</u> This is the tricky part,
especially if it's someone you work with
daily or live next door to or in the same
building or floor. And for god sake don't
write insulting emails, texts or
letters to your supervisors or Human
Resources or landlord from your office
computer. If the person is tech savvy or
related to Someone higher up in the company
it could come back and bite you in the ass.

Make an appointment to see a Labor Attorney about the possible harassment, if the persons watching, they may back off. Worse case, they might have already infiltrate your emails at home and at work, this happens more than you think. So watch those anonymous emails.

5) <u>Once you become aware of the possible situation keep a journal of the events as they happen</u> change your passwords every 3-5 days snd take different routes to work and for god sake. And just for kicks when your walking to and from anywhere stop and take a casual look around. Scan the area around for familiar faces, cars, trucks, vans or anything out of the ordinary. Remember stalkers want to be close to you, and they love to watching you, what they hate more than anything is being watched.
To them that's just plain ole creepy, how ironic?.

Once you identify stalker, concentrate on letting them know that your aware of there presence, remember what I said earlier, "Fear is a powerful weapon". The simplest deterrent I've found is taking there picture, for some reason it does something to them emotionally. And after taking the photo make sure you email it to your mom or dad or someone you can really trust. The truth about stalker situations is the more your informed the better you can protect yourself. And something else, you can't see whats around you with your face planted in the rearview mirror putting on makeup or lipstick. If your driving down the street with the same route daily change your routine now and again, some of the best way's to recognize a tail is to change your routes daily.

Sometimes doing the unexpected can give you a heads up on the dirt bags in tow, or if time permits break free while you're at work and call a Car Rental Company that delivers. Meet the sale person away from your job and leave your car in the parking lot. Then when they leave you follow them, this seems to give some of them the Hebee Gebee's, this works well on simple minded stalkers, but not Psychopaths. Now, it's time to talk about the real deal so sit down so you can to take it all in. When I was an officer starting out in the system, I dealt with a lot of men convicted of sexual offenses, some I would never talk about or repeat. In the military when you form a battle plan you plan for as much as possible, that means all scenarios including failure, we call this <u>prepared readiness</u>. The art of being prepared for just about anything is important, and though we can never be prepare for everything it's important to put the odds in your favor as much as possible. Sometimes calling the police does absolutely nothing but you can hope, and sometimes telling you boss only make's it worse. Now suddenly, the freak has broken into you home stole your panties, urinated on your bed and just posted a hacked video of you on-line having sex with your new boyfriend. And to top it off, he's pissed off and your now getting death threats. Well…2 things to remember before you leave town. You can run from bullies but you can't hide and secondly, eventually they always find you. So remember:

1) <u>Remember the journal</u> The purpose of

The journal was to establish the first leg of

your possible legal defense when or if it come to that.

Trust me if it's gotten this far I can

assure you, the rain my friend…will soon fall.

Find the nearest internet cafe bring all your evidence so

you scan it and place it on a flash drive

in a PDF format. Take that flash drive and

send it to a relative or a friend. If you don't have one an even better option is a local victims rights counselor. At most Crisis Center's, counselors are there to assist you, but if possible you should search for someone with a Dr in front of there name....get it)

2) <u>Don't make it easy</u> Get lost in the crowd, that may be pretty hard with that pink unicorn hanging off your rearview mirror. Once you've established that the threat is real you now have 2 options, go off the grid or fight back, and don't be fooled People thats it. Remember, if the police were interested they'd have done something by now, and for the police there needs to be a crime of sorts committed. So, that time now, you either gonna run or <u>release the beast</u> either way the choice is yours. When releasing the beast you must first remember this is a life or death situation, why, because you

only have roughly 3 go arounds with the

cops before your labeled a nuisance caller.

(someone who abuses the 911 system with

Numerous phone calls that they can

legally do nothing about) Most police

department have codes that accompany

these people so the officer knows there chronic callers.

Once labeled, you'll more than likely never be

removed. This means every-time you call from that phone

line or that address they'll more than likely

Be drag there feet all the way to your home.

(The exception of course being when the

stalker breaks into your house).

When this happens you are truly on

your own, I mean it, so here's what you do

and this is only in an emergency.

1) Arm your self You can buy a gun and

learn how to use it, but most states have a

cool down period for hand guns, but if you

Live in the Great State of Alabama like I do

rifles and <u>shot guns will work and no cool down period</u>.

There a sweet form of defense and most of time

you can leave with it when you buy it.

There are also private sales that you can buy

your gun from a private owner, however

you should check your states laws.

Many give you a grace period when you

have to register the sale. Remember gun

laws were meant for law abiding citizens,

not criminals. Criminals my friend could care less.

2) <u>Learn how to use it</u> In most states

carrying an unlicensed hand gun is a

felony, but remember in many state a 12

gauge shot gun (a.k.a Street Sweeper) or a

hunting rifle in the trunk is totally

legal. I can assure you that a Mossburg with

pistol grips and an infrared scope, yeah!

that's a true attention getter. And

After all, as a Bail Bondsman it has always

been my weapon of choice.

3) <u>Keep it loaded</u> An empty gun is a total waste of time. Who does that!

4) <u>As soon as you can go legal</u> Get the license and register the guns it helps improve your successful self-defense claim along with all the other information. Remember your going to have to prove you were in imminent danger when everything goes down. Having and unregistered gun in your car, house or purse for months is not a benefit without practice, thats just stupid. Now, depending on where you live you maybe in the clear but remember your due diligence. If you don't have the heart to stay and fight I suggest you get on the road but before you start singing happy trails you may want to make a few lifestyle changes first, so listen very carefully.

1) <u>Always assume that the person stalking</u>

<u>you has all of your personal information</u>
Your social security number and drivers license information. There are web site on the internet that specialize in selling this information to anyone with a credit card. There are actual case's were the stalker has used stolen credit cards from victim to track down the victim down. By using the victims stolen card information it looks as though the victim is crazy and fabricating a false reports. One of the favorite defense's used by Attorneys is to blame the victim.

2) <u>No more plastic strictly cash</u> If you've been going through this nightmare for any amount of time, you should have already known this day could come. So everything you have should be converted into cash as soon as possible. If you truly have no place to fall back to, try mom and dads at least there you know the lay of the land.

Lastly, this is a situation of extremes, which means that you have exhausted every known legal resource. That means the word legal, no longer applies if it's a life or death situation, so it's time to choose. Make sure you keep written and audio records of everything, the State will try to have most of this thrown out but save your documentation. Judge's feel sympathy for victims that did everything they could within the bounds of the law, so do jury's, so try your best to stay within those bounds. When going off grid remember the less things you have in your name the better. Everything today is tracked by Cyberhoods, and thanks to the Patriot Act it's only getting worse. Try not to buy new cars or move into fancy apartment complex's, off the grid means simple living, so keep it simple. The best way I've found to do this is when you move away, find a roommate that has already established a utility profile. This way they'll be no need for credit checks and digital foot prints that follow you. Stay off Facebook and other social media for a while, the down time and will give you time to reflect. Try to remember your conversations with friends and other's so when your traveling you can keep your stories straight, and always's go place's that others would never expect.

The Politics
of
A Failing Society

Phrase of the day

If poverty is the result of poor choices, then wealth is the result of and blind ambition. Which gave birth…to Capitalism.

Through out the past 50 years we Americans have under gone some type of rebirth so to speak. A period in which certain beliefs we had aren't quite the same beliefs we still have. For example, Gay marriage, hey people times are changing along with Religious acceptance of Muslims and women taking the role of head of household. Even the pledge of allegiance is now considered taboo in this day and age, who knew?. So, what happen to us, and why the sudden change in society and our hearts, even more crazy now is the hatred for our Government. It's like for some reason we really seem happy trying to kill each other and everyone else around us for the slightest disagreement.

But why, Is it likely that most of us have this new feeling of awkwardness in society, or is it more likely that like something in our new capitalistic society has changed us. Have we lost our faith in God and religion or has religion become just another form of capitalism, where God is competing with our money. I once had a college instructor tell me "A true capitalist will find anyway to make buck, no matter how said or disgusting". Maybe it's because everytime you turn on the television there's a politician yelling and screaming insults and things like "That's the American way". But as sad as it may seem are our moral values being repro-grammed by our political views. Have we bought so much into the ideal of them versus us simply because we have different views. I find myself sometimes getting carried away with politic's, not because it makes sense, but because politicians seem to say the right things at the right time. Everybody's a messiah when times are hard, and when your desperate you'll listen to anything. Insults, accusations and false claims are always attempts to create unrest and anarchy in our society an destabilize unity. Seems there's never a shortage of sell out's willing to do or say anything so he or she can make a few bucks. The 21 century has opened our eye's on every frontier except one, the blame game of politics, and many of you know exactly what I'm talking about. They're those people who can never take responsibility for there own actions because it's always easier to blame someone else, the Government's to blame or the White man or even those Mexicans crossing the border. We're all responsible and believe me there enough fault for everybody, the Democrats, the Republicans but most of all us The American people. We're all responsible for this so call mad house political society were living in today. Now it's not completely safe to say that every Republican wants to turn back the hands of time 100 years to slavery. But when it comes to Liberals, there are those who do quite frankly take it a little to far with the whole Government rules thing. Look, if you feel you got hustled in 2008 on election night with "Change we can believe in" guess what, so did everybody else. So suck it up and stop blaming the hustler and blame yourself . The Politicians of America, politely known as the "Do as I say, and not as I do crowd" have managed to unleash an apocalyptic on slot of grifters and political pimps into our society controlling all aspects of our financial futures. What we know in America as the Double Standard a.k.a Capitalism has become the inspiration for the largest crime wave in our country's history, White Collar Fraud. But what is white collar fraud, and what's the difference between fraud and business, and why has it left such devastating effect on both our economy and our personal lives. In order to understand it we must first understand that politics that gave way to it. I mean the very law makers that you and I voted for, who created the loop holes in the law's giving these cretans an opportunity to run amuck. So honestly who's fault is it really? Before we can begin to understand how to fix America, we must first realize that we live in a world of frauds, yes I said it, and yes I mean't it. And after all, I'm a Bail Bondsman and I should know. The fact is that we as Americans trust people way to much, way WAY to much. For some reason we've been taught to believe the poor people have no credibility while rich people speak the words of God. That you can trust any man in a $10,000 suit, more so than a man wearing a pair of blue jeans. Really? As a Bail bondsman I've seen every kind of criminal there is and let me say all of them suits and all were pure garbage. Many cons will use the race card like a credit card to gain an edge or two on any consumers with a pulse as long as they get what they want. The truth is you've all been hoodwinked into believing that some educated low life with a college degree could knows more from reading a few text books than you could ever learn from a life of hard knocks, and that's the truth. The fact is many of you have learned things the hard way, expensive yes, painful yes, but you've learned. And sometimes this might just be the best way to educate some people, but like my doctor said in her infinite wisdom "That's just my opinion, you should get a second one". So the question is why can't we trust people? Even more frightening are our own relatives, shouldn't those be the one's we should be able to trust the most? Well I'm here to answer the tough questions folks and here it is HELL NO!! And let me tell you why, when we were born we all have some instinctive form of judgment, although not completely developed at birth, it's still there and it does work. Think of it this way, when your 2 year old does something wrong you instinctively say "No" and most of the time that works. You see the word "No" triggers a response for your 2 year old to either run like hell or to let the tears fall. Now here's the funny part, turn your back for 10 seconds and they'll do it again until you turn back around and then they'll instinctively stop. As primitive as it sounds it still demonstrates the ability the reason. Which is exactly my point, how did 61% of you lose your ability to reason in an the last election year. Think about it, reasoning doesn't take intelligence, it simply takes a little common sense, and listening ability which is something we all have but many seldom us. But instead of using your brains you trust some stranger on television to think for you, like lambs to slaughter as if to following his/her words like the words of God. I'm going to give you 2 examples of blind trust, this is not to scare you, but to make you aware that you are responsible for your own actions. When it comes to money, property, health, children or investments in the eye's of the court's you should have know better than to follow blind trust. In the Great State Of Alabama we have something called Due Diligence which basically means you have an obligation to go the extra mile to insure that the person you give your hard earned money to is actually reputable. Just the simple concept of a being handed a business card by a guy in and a nice suit just doesn't cut it as an excuse for you handing over your life savings. It is the responsibility of the consumer to assure a satisfactory outcome by doing Due Diligence, a.k.a. doing your homework.

This should be done on each and every transaction that you conduct with a potential business partner or store owner. Here's a few scenarios. Many years ago my wife and I were house hunting in Dothan Alabama and found a beautiful 1920's home in what was soon to be rezoned as a historic district. The home needed some work but we thought we could breathe life back into a piece of history. When we called the number we spoke with a female realtor that quickly transferred us to an older gentleman. He stated that the home was for sale but he wasn't showing it to anyone because he had and investor who wanted to buy it for cheap and he wanted to teach the owner a lesson. Apparently the elderly woman who own the property wanted the home to go to a good family with children but he had an Investor friend who wanted to buy the property and was cutting him in on a piece of the action. Now apparently the owner dismissed his friends offer and he took offense to it and made it personal. So out of protest he was tanking the sale of the home to a family to force the sale to his investor friend. The poor lady had no idea the the real estate contract she signed gave the realtor absolute discretion over the offers that could or could not be presented to her for her own property. Like I said, to much trust. Now we'll move on to the second example. A young ladies father she hadn't spoken into in almost 10 years died leaving her his only living heir. Since her mother was no longer married to her father she was forced to make the tough call of pulling the plug on his life support and ending his life. After which she discovered being his only living relative someone had to take responsibility for her fathers estate. So she graciously excepted the job and started liquidating the estate only to discovered her father was in serious debt. Regardless of the circumstances she continued to do her best to bring the estate back into the black. One step of course, was to sell the home he owned, so she hired a real estate agent to do what she thought was to list the home for sale. The problem lie's in the distance, you see because the home was located in another state over 2000 miles away she put blind trust in the Real Estate agent's ability to sell the home. As it turns out she got totally scammed. A week or two later she received a call from a friend of her passing father, seems while drive by he noticed her father's old furniture out on the curb of the street. Thinking the worse he called to ask her what was happening with the house, she was later shock to discover that the Real Estate agent had given a key to the home buyer 5 weeks before closing on the home. Seems the buyer was a investor friend of the Real Estate Agent and they were trying to avoid paying state taxes and stamps on the flip. So she secretly allowed the buyer to begin renovating the home without the seller's permission. Because she the seller, was living over 2000 miles away, the buyer begin ripping out cabinets, toilets and sinks in the home before he even closed or owned the home. He was literally gutting the inside of the entire home on the down low without her knowledge and the Real Estate agent was in on the whole thing. It was only by a freak accident when the friend of her fathers called alarmed at what he saw, that she found out about the renovations. Needless to say the agent denied giving him a key but failed to mention she gave the buyer the code to the lock box instead. This gave him unlimited access to any and everything within the home and because of the distance he decided to beat the system. But here's the real problem. Until the closing actually took place she still owned the home. As a result of the renovation attempt, she lost the deal on the house because the buyer ran into a unexpected expenses. Seems during the non existing renovation, he ran into a few problems that would cost more than he wanted. In doing so he decide he wanted to re-negotiate the price or walk away and leave the home mangled and gutted. When she refused, the Real Estate agent called her back to inform her the buyer was pulling out of the deal if she didn't lower the price. Remember this is a probate sale case and she was using the proceeds to clear claims against her father's estate. Because of the Real Estate agent's shady deal on the side with the buyer and the seller's inexperience of Real Estate agents, she not only lost the house but got screwed by the Probate lawyer as well. Bottom line the whole thing ended in disaster both financially and emotionally and believe it or not what the Real Estate agent did was totally legal in her state. Learn from this people ....learn. There's nothing worse than being caught off guard by a bunch of low life two timing crooks that have nothing but bad intentions....Period.

Our Court System

Is Justice for all? or the great divide

Words to live by

Its obvious that anyone that tells you "Take one for the team" is completely oblivious of the meaning of self sacrifice.

Truth is we all enter the world the same way, cold scared, half blind and totally and completely pissed off. With the first breath we take and the opening of our eye's, we celebrate the beginning of life with the awkwardness of child birth. As our lives come together, our new beginning starts with a the warm touch and the familiar sounds of our mother's heart beat. These loving gestures by mothers everyday all over the world signal our acceptance as we are lovingly welcomed as new members of the human race. For a child who's spent 9 months in there mother's womb, it's that heart beat that comforts and assure's us as our live's begin. Our world is constantly and forever evolving, with new technologies, new ideas, new discoveries that often places many people under unconceivable stress.

But never fear my friends because we as Americans have a secret weapon, a weapon with such power that it can bring our enemies to there knees both physically and financially. What is this weapon you may ask? Well it's Lawyers. Yes.. Just think when ever your feeling down and out and you suddenly have the urge to go let's say, go homicidal and shoot a dozen or more people or rape a bus load of cheer leaders, it pays to have a good defense lawyer on speed dial. This way you can always count on your Lawyer's expert ability to us some bullcrap excuse to try to justify the horrific act you committed with some half ass legal defense. But has our legal system become nothing more than a green light for crime, and are some crimes done just because we can get away with them? Which bring us to my next point, are some legal defense's just excuse's for deliberate acts of violence against people? And if we continue on this path will we inherently be creating a new form of legal system for a society built on legal excuse's for the next generation of sociopaths? If so we call this shop and go crime, the way to buy your way out prison but the legal term for it is actually Premeditated murder. Why, because you thought about it First. Even with all the hoopla accompanied with our present legal system we must first remember that one cardinal rule. Courts don't right wrongs, they enforce laws. I'll say it again for all of those who road the short bus to school. Courts don't right wrongs…period! The facts is in some ways the court's hinder justice, and we'll discuss several ways how these actions may occur later. Blaming the victim In most sexual assault cases is the most common, in fact blaming the victim is the number one defense used in most sexual assault cases today. Which beg the question, "Why do we often blame the victim for what happens to them personally". If someone gets sick we say it's there lifestyle that's to blame, If someone becomes over weight or gets cancer some try to justify that by blaming a persons diet, or power limes, or additives in their food. So what's the deal, and why do we as American have to establish blame. In domestic violence cases you will often hear the husband say "She hit me first, or "I was just defending myself". Whether it be truthful or not, seldom will you hear the the man admit that he got carried away in anger and went to far. Let's say he decided to used a bat to break his wife's arm or give her a broken jaw or better yet provide some missing teeth. I had a guy I knew way back years ago tell his girl friend "Everytime you say something to me stupid I'm going to knock out a tooth". Now as ridiculous as it sounded he kept true to his words, and after roughly 5 months of a nightmare dating relationship with this guy, the last count was she had roughly 5 teeth left. I noticed that she had such lower self esteem afterwards that she barely left the house most of the time. I would asked a friend a couple of years later after I moving away what happen to her, he said sadly that she committed suicide. By the end of there relationship she was toothless, homeless, and her nose had been broken 3 times, her jaw was broken twice and it was all to much for her to bare. In the end the law did nothing to save this woman, her teeth or her life. And so the great debate continues, should the Government get involved in the personal affairs of people's lives. Well when it comes to Domestic Violence I say yes, when it come to sexual assault and child abuse I say yes, and there're many reasons why. You have to remember that the number one excuse used by these type's of men is "It's not my fault". Simply put, ask any Drug Addict that robs a convenience store clerk an shoots her at pointe blank range and he'll tell you it's wasn't him, it was the drugs. The drugs he voluntarily took on his own accord, the drugs he purchased with the money he received after killing her, and I'm sick of accuse's. I remember bailing a guy out once that told me " I tried so hard not to hit her, but she just wouldn't stop talking ". Then there's the infamous " It hurts me to my heart to see your face like this, but you have to blame your self". Remember to a Domestic Violence abuser's he's never the problem, it's always the victim. We'll discuss this later but now were on courts and contracts. Now ladies, when it comes down to things like contracts you must remember one consistent element. "A contract may be used to circumvent a law, but seldom can the law be used to circumvent a contract". So for the purpose of arguments lets look at a landlord tenant example of a friend of mine, and remember I'm not a Lawyer. Now, depending on your state, the laws may be different so remember to consult an Attorney in your state. So let's look at two states I kinda familiar with Florida and Alabama. Just so you know again, I'm not a lawyer, but I could play one on T.V (Yeah…

right!). In the State of Florida when you rent and apartment you have the right to do a walk through, whenever you find something wrong, you document that item on something called an inspection report. Here's the kicker just because you document it doesn't mean the landlord has a legal right to fix it, it's his choice to fix or your to reject it. See, for some reason most people rarely read the fine print in these contracts and lately, some ambitious lawyers have started putting cash clauses in these leases limiting the responsibility of the landlord financially and making the renter the new cash cow.

You see a cash clause (That's what we call them here) limits the amount of damage's or repair's the landlord is liable for. For example. A couple of years ago I saw a lease that made the tenant responsible for any and all minor repairs under $1000.00 dollars (The key is minor and what defines minor). This included appliances, air conditioning, plumbing, electrical and e.t.c., The tenant misread the lease for being the landlord was responsible for any and all repairs under $1000.00 dollars and signed. Of course this was a private residence and by not paying attention he not only missed the clause, but he missed the most important part. Anything not repaired upon vacating the residence was the tenant responsibility, making the landlord responsible for nothing and the tenants financially responsible for everything. Needless to say because the tenant signed the lease with the clause in it, he was financially responsible for each repair minor repair in the unit. Simply put each repair was considered under the contract an individual repair. The landlord basically got the apartment repaired for free at the end of every lease, to this day he has yet to replaced anything in his units. But is this legal? Well.. who knows but it's a contract and it would cost money to challenge. And because it was signed by the tenant, most of the time it circumvents the law of landlord/tenant responsibility at least depending on the Judge that is. Because the tenant agreed in the contract to do the repairs himself for free there's was nothing really a Judge could ever do bar some miracle. Keeping in mind that every state is different you should really, yeah really take the time to read these written lease agreements ladies especially for private residences. Remember, in the end no one put a gun to your head and made you sign the lease agreement. You should also look out for Peeping Tom Clause. A Peeping Tom Clause is a clause where a landlord use's the right to inspect the premises as a open door policy to rummage through your personal things. There are hundreds of case's were landlords have rented private residences to women and installed hidden camera's as well as other deviant behavior. On famous case was in the State of California where a landlord would sneak into women's residence's while they were sleeping women and masterbate on top of them. The reason this struck me was because of the Peeping Tom Clause he couldn't be charged with breaking and Entering. The lease specifically stated that the landlord had the right to enter the premises at anytime, day or night without notice, and he did! He stole panties blouses and everything else he could fine. Lesson learn ladies, read, read, and read. <u>Mechanics and auto Repairs</u> are another one that can be a little tricky, let's face it, a good mechanic is hard to find but and a honest one is virtually impossible. Why, because the honest one's usually don't stay in business long, and let's face it honesty seldom pays the bills. The problem is with newer cars, the engine diagnostics can sometimes be a shot in the dark, or so they say. The fact is cars today are so high tech and cost so much money why would you ever take your car to anyone but a certified mechanic. Now I know the dealer can be expense and everyone complains about the dealership, but honestly I kinda like my Ford Dealer. But just because I like him doesn't't mean he won't bend me over the table ladies, if you know what I mean. And if he'll do that to me, he'll do it to you twice as fast. The truth is if your not paying attention a $200.00 repair can turn into a $2000.00 repair real quick. Here's what happen to my buddy. A friend of mine went to a dealership in the St Petersburg/ Clearwater Florida area for what was a simple oil change $34.99. The service writer would later call a say "We found a few problems that we need to address" over the phone he went over the list and they agreed on what needed to be fixed. After about an hour or so he gets another phone call from the same service writer saying "Look it's a lot worse than we thought I'm going to need your permission to fix this stuff or everything else we did will be useless". He then asked "what in gods name have you been doing to this car" my friend asked "What stuff, what's wrong " the service writer said and I quote" I really don't know, we won't know until we get into it". Now the word of the day boys and girls is "Gullible" which basically means in street terms "Chump" but my buddy though reluctant, agreed. Remember Service Writer's and Mechanics work on billable hours, and get a percentage of the total bill minus parts. The next morning we went to pickup his car to the tune of $4673.12 Needless to say he refused to pay the bill, but unfortunately for my friend, the dealer had a clause in his service agreement which he signed for just such occasions. The agreement stated that if the customer fail to pay the bill within 30 days the dealer would keep the vehicle and sell it in order to to pay the debt. However, the language in the contract was of course far more covert. My friend believing he was in the right and never reading the contract or the clause said "I'll see you in court". Now to make matters worse the clerk of court set a court date for more than 60 days down the road. Are we starting to see the picture forming here folks, needless to say not only did he lose the case but the Judge considered the car abandon. Even worse he still got stuck with the bill, all $4673.12 plus interest. Needless to say we car pooled for a little while. Every situation is course different ladies, so remember the basic rules when dealing with shifty service people. Never get distracted when reading contracts, agreements, warranties or anything that requires a time commitment or specific terms. One of the greatest tricks used by shady sales people is as soon as you start reading they begin asking you about your kids or something to distract you. 'Tell me about your kids, is this your first car purchase, where did you go to college". All of these are clever distractions techniques used by Real Estate, Car, Financial professionals, Insurance Agents and most importantly Closing Agents and Attorneys so you forget to pay attention. You should also remember one thing above all, no one's forcing you to sign the agreement, everything is a choice and you can leave at anytime. Remember a Hold Harmless Agreement is just that, that person is held harmless from any legal liability, so read before you sign. Also, when buying a vehicle, never pay your down payment to any car dealer before the deal is complete and you see the financing terms. Remember it's your money the last thing you do is hand over the check, not the first thing. So we'll continue with contract scams. Recently there has been a major influx of bogus homes entering the market, many of these have been illegally foreclosed upon by banks and mortgage companies looking to turn a fast buck. A general red flag is something called a Special Warranty Deed, You should also be wary of any home purchases that may require a double contract (A standard Real Estate offer Contract and a Secondary Bank Contract which may actually be something similar to something called a hold harmless agreement). You should always consult with an Attorney who specializes in Real Estate law, if you can get your hands on the contract from the selling agent prior to signing. Some will give you the impression that it must be signed here and now but it doesn't't, and if you ever take the time to read this 15 page agreement you'll would probably go in shock. Just a brief summery of most of the one's that I've read from major banks clearly state that the offer has not officially been accepted until a non-refundable deposit has been received whether they accept the offer or not. We have a street name for these types of contracts, there called sucker contracts. Not only do they take your money but they explicitly say you agree not to sue if you by chance discover after the sale that they the bank didn't't actually own the property, gotta those love conservative capitalist. You see in some states you can have as much as 2 years to sue someone for an illegal transaction, after all, selling a home you don't really own and issuing a title you printed on a canon printer is a felony.. <u>But not for a bank.</u> You see this is where that scam regarding contracts and laws get's really blurred, so you need to remember:

**A contract may be used to circumvent a law, but seldom can the law be used to circumvent a contract". Which basically means regardless of what the law say's there are only a handful of legal defenses that can be used for voiding or breaking a contract. Heres and example. You bought a home for $168,000.00 cash you figure you'll sink your retirement savings into the purchase so when you get to sunny Florida you can drive that new golf cart off into the sunset. Heres the play, if that house was illegally foreclosed upon by the mortgage company the previous owner could still have standing as much as 2 years after the transaction. Which means while your watching the sunset from your back porch, someone could knock at the door from the sheriff Department, and politely welcoming you to sunny Florida with a summons. When you get to court the former owner says that the foreclosure was illegal because the bank hoodwinked them and never proved ownership. Remember the law normally doesn't works for both side's, it's the Plaintiff or the Defendant that's how it was originally setup by our forefathers. Depending on the judge, and this is the beauty of America, it can go either way. The bad news is if it goes against you, you'll have to vacate the premisses at a total loss. However in the Great state of Alabama where I reside there is no foreclosure defense. What this means is the mortgage company is not obligated to show proof to any courts, unless of course you challenge the foreclosure in the court's. This means the burden of proof is on you not them, but along with the burden of proof comes the expense of court. Unfortunately theres not a lot of Attorneys that will help you fight a bogus foreclosure and for the ones that do is a 50/50 shot that there just taking your money. But have faith my friend, the number of good Attorney's entering the Great State of Alabama I'm happy to say is on the rise. Every year a new stock of ambitious young Bucks an Doe's enter the legal arena to fighting for there chance to make a honest difference in the world. And let's be honest, if you've lived in a house for 3 years and not payed a dime to your mortgage company you should be able to come up with $5000- $10,000 grand to fight your case. Truly…nobody can afford to work for free. Nobody!!!! So how could you expect your

Attorney to. Everyone at on time or another falls on hard times but we all have an obligation to get back up and keep fighting, anything else is just Un-American. Next up, car sales. What is it about cars and Stupid people. First let me say that I refuse to go into great detail on this subject because for me, this as in most other case's, is just plain ole common sense. So here we go, If you buy a used car from anyone in most of the lower 48 States, unless other wise written not <u>orally stated</u> written, that my friend is more than likely a as-is sale, Period. One of my favorite show is The Peoples Court not for just the legal aspect, however that's pretty good too, but for the shear stupidity of the plaintiffs suing. The fact is people, you can't make up this kind of ignorance. So with this brief section I hope to keep you future litigants from sounding like complete retards and misfits.

Senario 1

If someone tells you that a 1974 Pinto, they tell you that it runs perfect with no problems, totally taken care of, all they ever had to do was change the oil that my friend is probably a lie. An if someone say's it hurts them to there heart to let it go for let's say $2500.00 because there dead grand mother gave it to them on her death bed, Well my friend anythings possible. But if your stupid enough to believe a car recalled for exploding when hit from the rear because of the gas tank, not to mention countless other recalls runs perfectly with no problems for the last 40 years you my friend need psychiatric help.

Senario 2

If you buy and 91 Chevy Citation sedan off of Craig's list and they're asking $500.00 for because all it needs is a little TLC, common sense should make you ask " If all it needs is a little work why not keep it". And if there response is " Well I would but it just doesn't excite me any more" thats probably a lie. Why, it's a 1991 Citation sedan and honestly how exciting can it be for any person to be driving a 1991 sedan. I mean really if you can afford excitement maybe you should cut back on the excitement and buy a car that actually works. So don't bother suing when the engine blows.

In Closing, When you decide to sue someone try to use a little common sense, really there's nothing sadder than someone blaming the government or someone else for there own stupidity. The Government has become the fall guy for every ignorant form of stupidity, poverty, wealth grabbing and everything in between. And yet know one is willing to face the truth, because we put these nut jobs into public office. We as Americans have created our own hardships and have yet to live up to the expectations of our own founding father's. If anyone will honestly acknowledge the facts, thew would see the problems not the government..it's us. The truth is we are the government. So to recap.

**Read all contracts completely I don't care how long it takes Never assume anything, assumption is nothing more than a collapsing foundation for success. Always ask questions and if what they say is not in the written agreement insist they put it in because if isn't in writing, it never happened.

**Don't get distracted or side tracked by small meaningless gabbing when signing contacts. If your reading and signing contracts and the person presenting the contracts suddenly finds themselves in a time crunch, honestly…that's there problem!! If they Insist you just sign blindly you should walk away.

**Don't assume because you're working with family that you won't get jacked

**Due diligence always pays's (always think fraud until you Know differently)

**If it's to good to be true…..people, it usually is!!! Sleep on it first, but if you can't, beware of deals that last less than 5 Minutes or that are quote "once in a lifetime"

**Don't sign any document or commit to any agreement spontaneously. Spontaneous works great for sex and dinning out at restaurants, but has devastating on your finances. Even though we all make bad decisions now and then, the truth is it's not the responsibility of the courts to get you out of poor decisions. Getting screwed by a contractor is common, so common in fact that a lot of states have adopted legislation to stay out of these types of disputes. So how do you know if your about to get screwed…well, you don't. There have been cases where contractors have had all the right references, licenses and insurances and have still walked off of a job sticking the homeowner for thousands. And the police depending on the state and city you live in could be a total waste of time because they only know 2 words to recite…Civil Matter. And we should always remember that the word <u>no</u> is not discriminatory. Yes I said it. Now I know my fellow brothers and sister won't like this but, just because a white person at a business establishment tells you no to something it doesn't constitute discrimination. Even though your feelings were hurt, the word "No" still Isn't considered discrimination. I know, if that were the case I should have sued my parents for millions. Even if someone use's of the "N" word it's not enough for a lawsuit as hurtful as it is so please take the time to consult an attorney before filing nuisance lawsuits through the courts.

The conclusion's of
what we've learn

We've reached the end my friend

I can remember just like yesterday a conversation I once had with a true serial killer. During our conversation he said something that I'll never forget. He told me "<u>God may send you out into the world, but it's the devil that'll lead me to you</u>". I thought to myself, what a powerful message to give to someone. Before I started on my books, my wife and I decide to take a quest. That quest would lead us to over 30 states through out the great USA, and let me be frank when I say, some truly scary people. Like it's written in the good book 'I send out as sheep among wolves'. I ask myself sometimes did god know more than he let on. I was never really big into the whole holy spirit thing, it's hard to believe in things you can't see sometimes, especially when it's somethings we can't see or touch. But that's faith, and faith after all is the belief in things unseen. Through my travels I've remained as low key as I could, not hiding out but watching. Not me, but you and there's one thing I've learn over these last 4 years on the road. Most of you have no heart, no not the one in your chest, but the one that controls your will. I've met so manny good people along the way, and I'm amazed how easily many of you were swayed by the less admirable. As I said earlier were all born with morals, but despite what any of you think you don't actually lose them, you simply let someone else convince you there irrelevant. Listen, all morals are relevant, we need them to survive and guide us in ways our instincts could never understand. When your sitting next to someone at a lunch table and they say "Wow she looks fat in that dress" or " Hide your purse look who's coming" you feel bad, at least I do. And that's a good thing because it means when the devils talking to you, you realize that it's the Devil testing you. When people pickup everything the own and move a 100 miles from everybody, there doing it for a reason. The simple fact is, most of the time there in pain, and being alone helps them process there pain. Don't interfere, just allowing them to live in peace could help. Living that way maybe good for them because there honestly, there no good to the rest of us.

You see, human beings are social creatures, and if someone can't stand being round other people, then he or she becomes a risk to the everyone. I will also ask all of you when traveling from place to place to write down your thought's, I do and often, it helps me when dealing with cynical people. It makes it a lot easier to handle and much easier to digest. The old saying that misery loves company is oh so true, and if you notice all unhappy people require an audience. But don't you be that audience, stay focused on the positive road and you'll find yourself a happier healthier person for it. Our bodies are nothing but biological vessels in life, there only mean't to take us so far. The rest however is up to you, because your spirit live on. My father use to say that in any septic tank it's not the water on the top you have to worry about, but It's the crap at the bottom that kills you. Even when keeping all that in mind, why is it always the greenest part of the lawn thats the shittiest. Maybe it's because for some reason, some of the the nastiest place's can sometimes yield some of the most beautiful things. But the important part is that we as human beings can always learn something. I once heard a sermon from a pastor who described the job of the Devil.

As he began going down the list of things I realized something, The Devil is truly a busy person. And when you have that much work that needs to be done, you need a lot of recruits. It's why our world is full of skeptic's, cynics and non-believers, not to forget sabotage, alienators and down right angry people. When I set out on my journey I knew about the criminal element, But what I was looking to discover was the human element. I wanted to see if there's was still any humanity left in America, and if there was, is it thriving or dying. As I've changed my life personally, I found it highly necessary to purge myself of negativity from my life and you should do the same. Family, friends, co-workers it's just not healthy to allow people to effect you in a negative way. The moral of this story is pretty simple, just because a person's not locked up in jail, doesn't mean there a good person. Some infractions people commit are not criminal, but ethical or moral in nature. You must know when to tow the line and when to walk away. As mothers you have the duty of raising your children in the best possible way to ensure they have futures. Honestly the way things are going, the future's not so bright for most of them. I left The Department of Correction for a reason, That reason was nobody can stay in that environment and not have the residue of criminals,Scumbags and Misfits not rub off on them. It just can't be done, you will eventually believe that everybody is a lying piece of crap and you'll start to hate everyone and begin lose your faith.

Purging yourself of that type of environment helps a person reconnect with themselves and there faith along with there family, but in a completely different way. I've learned that the first person to hurl the first insult is usually the person with the biggest skeleton in there closet. They're normally the first person with the most insecurity and a lot of times the person with the most baggage to carry around. Insults are nothing more than a psychological defense mechanism used by people who don't have the courage to deal with there own problems. Many of them lack confidence so much that they've turned to the public humiliation of others in hopes of getting a laugh. If any of you have ever dealt with bullies everything's fine as long as there hurling the insults your way, but when you hurl one back they always seem to come undone. This is because of there fragile nature. I'm hoping you ladies learned something, especially when it comes to dating and finance's. I hope you learn it's ok to fall in love, just be smart about it. And most of all, I hope you mom's have a better Idea of Sexual Predators, not only what to look for but how to protect you children. In the end if I can help save one child, one woman or prevent one of you from being scammed, if feel I would have truly done my job. Thank you and good luck.

www.ingramcontent.com/pod-product-compliance
Lightning Source LLC
Chambersburg PA
CBHW081418090426
42738CB00017B/3401